D1582278

William, Earl of Craven

& The Art of Photography

Noel Chanan

HALSGROVE

First published in Great Britain in 2006

British Library Cataloguing-in-Publication Data
A CIP record for this title is available from the British Library

ISBN 1 84114 491 6
ISBN 978 1 84114 491 7

HALSGROVE

Halsgrove House
Lower Moor Way
Tiverton, Devon EX16 6SS
Tel: 01884 243242
Fax: 01884 243325
email: sales@halsgrove.com
website: www.halsgrove.com

Printed and bound by Industrie Grafiche Spa, Italy

Photography: David Golby
Design: Sharon O'Inn

For June,
my companion on the journey through photography

For Benjamin,
to whom I promised the story of his pioneering ancestor

VIRTUS IN ACTIONE CONSISTIT

Contents

Prologue

Towards the end of 1998, one of the directors of Bearne's Fine Art Auctioneers of Exeter brought in for assessment and possible sale a number of elephant folios of 'old photographs' belonging to a client. With no resident expert in photography, but recognising the works as being of unusually fine quality, and with the experienced auctioneers' nose for a good thing, Bearne's invited myself and an old friend and colleague, the artist and connoisseur of nineteenth century photography, Graham Ovenden, to inspect the contents of the folios and advise. Ovenden and I met with Bearne's then directors, Robin Barlow and the late Brian Bearne, at their salerooms, on 7th December 1998 . The several huge and weighty folios were laid out on trestle tables ready for us and we immediately set about sorting through them, attended by a mounting sense of excitement. The photographic prints that were revealed were generally of an exceptionally deep sepia-aubergine-black hue, for the most part in fine original condition, many of them mounted on card embossed with a noble crest. They were the master-works of an English amateur of the 1850s, whose work was hitherto totally unknown to historians of photography. The name attached to the folios was that of William, 2nd Earl of Craven (1809–66). At final count there were fifty-eight mainly large-scale works by Craven (plus a handful of duplicates and a few lesser pieces) some mounted on card, as well as Craven's collection of the works of a dozen of his leading contemporaries. These included the pioneer of wet-plate photography, Frederick Scott Archer, and the great English master, Roger Fenton; of French photographers, Charles Marville, Count Olympe Aguado and most notably, Gustave Le Gray. This last was represented by nine of his seascapes, one of the largest known extant groups of these wondrous images. All in all, an astounding discovery.

Ovenden being much preoccupied at the time with his painting, it finally fell to myself, by general agreement, to prepare the works for sale, under the watchful eye of Robin Barlow. Aware that Craven's photographs might be dispersed into private collections and that the name of this great pioneer might return to its recent obscurity, I asked the indulgence of Bearne's in allowing me to write an essay-length foreword to the sale catalogue, which might at least provide a point of reference for future historians of photography. It turned out to be no small task, since this once vastly wealthy family of ancient lineage had, in the early decades of the twentieth century, fallen on difficult times; wealth and estates greatly diminished, name all but consigned to oblivion, and documents for the most part beyond the reach of even the most persistent of researchers.

By the time the catalogue was due to go to press my interest in Craven had become near obsessive and I continued my researches. Eventually, they bore fruit. I came upon a number of photocopies made twenty years earlier of images—so I was told by an official of the institution in which I discovered them—taken from a borrowed album containing photographs by the 3rd Earl of Craven and compiled in 1866, his title and the date being scribbled, at the time of copying, on the margin of a portrait. From the age of the subject it was immediately obvious that this was an error. The photograph was actually a self-portrait of William, the 2nd Earl, taken somewhat earlier than 1866. With luck on my side, I managed to follow the tortuous trail back to its source, and was at last rewarded by the rediscovery of William Craven's masterpiece, a massive and ornate album containing many additional images, inscribed with the title *A Record of the Earl of Craven's Photographic Experiments*. The album was sold at Bearne's—intact—in May 2001, a year after the sale of the folios.

Both auctions were immensely exciting events and brought rewards beyond expectation. As for myself, I had the satisfaction of seeing Craven take his rightful place amongst his peers, recognised as the master photographer that he undoubtedly was.

Very little documentation has survived of the Craven estates. A large part of what exists is to be found in the Craven Papers held at the Bodleian Library, Oxford, where the most useful material for the purposes of this work consists in the surviving travel diaries of Lady Emily Mary Craven, née Grimston, daughter of the First Earl of Verulam, wife of William, 2nd Earl of Craven. The Countess of Craven was also a prolific writer of letters, in particular to her sister Katharine, Countess of Clarendon, called 'Kate'. Part of this correspondence is catalogued amongst the Papers of Lady Katharine Clarendon, also at the Bodleian. Crucially, however, no letters have come to light from Emily Mary to Kate dating from the early 1850s. Since they were in constant contact throughout that decade as well as before and after, and the letters generally contain what might now pass in a daily phone call between loving sisters, a large tranche of material must be presumed lost, unless it lies elsewhere, undiscovered.[i] To a limited extent we are rescued by Kate. She kept copious diaries throughout her adult life, though some of those dating from the early 'fifties are also missing. Kate's husband, George Villiers, 4th Earl of Clarendon, was Foreign Secretary throughout much of the 1850s, of which the central years were dominated by the Crimean War, and literally ninety-five per cent of Kate's extensive writings consist in detailed and fascinating accounts of the politicians and politics of the day, in which she was deeply immersed. But the few entries of a more intimate nature, including those referring to the Cravens, are telling; and Kate's is the only voice in the 1850s that mentions her brother-in-law's photography.

In Craven's own hand precious little survives—two or three brief notes addressed to his cousin Lady Caroline Fitzhardinge Maxse relating to the sad death of his youngest brother, Frederick, are in the Maxse archives. But of his photography—the

---

[i] Or is irretrievable - The Bodleian has a folio of water-damaged material that is beyond accessibility.

great camera and the photographic wagon, the lenses specially computed to fit them, glass for plates, paper for printing, card for mounting, chemicals for processing, nothing remains, not a bill, nor record of a transaction. Of notes on processes or reflections on his experimental work, not a leaf. Most regrettable of all, of the correspondence that one would like to imagine passing between Craven and other photographers—Archer, Fenton, Le Gray, there is not a word. Such dearth of original documentation is common to the lives of most of the pioneering photographers. Yet almost alone amongst his contemporaries, Craven's photographic journey is autobiographical, revolving around his life, family, forebears, and the home he loved. Towards the end of the nineteenth century photography as autobiography would become a commonplace; in the 1850s it was all but unknown. In the work of most of Craven's photographic colleagues we see only what they created; in Craven we perceive not only the images, but the man himself.

The results of further research have enabled the present text to be expanded well beyond the scope of the previous catalogue introductions, and new material has emerged allowing the correction of those errors that crept into the previous texts. Craven's story is also now set against a background of the birth of photography in 1839, in the shape of the daguerreotype; and the narrative endeavours to explain why the daguerreotype failed to carry photography forward into the 1850s, the decade in which the Art of Photography truly blossomed; this was Craven's decade. Unless and until further documents (or photographs) come to light, I hope that this may be considered so far as possible a substantive account of the life and work of William, 2nd Earl of Craven, Photographer.

Noel Chanan

9

A Portrait of William Craven

Entwined within William Craven's personal cypher is to be found a symbolic, though doubtless unintended, description of the man. The cypher, with its somewhat Germanic feel—the style being suggestive of Dürer's monogram—is an ingeniously fashioned encryption of the letters making up the name Craven, mirrored, *recte et retro*, structured like the two halves of the brain, each with its functions, conjoined by the *corpus callosum*, the bundle of nerves common to both parts, as is the upright of the letter E at the centre of the cypher. On the left side is to be found the traditional man, the conformist; on the right, the introspective one, the romantic, the artist. In Craven, during his lifetime, to all outward appearances, the left side was dominant.

William, 2nd Earl of Craven, by Alfred D'Orsay, 1843.

Of the surviving portraits, made just over twenty years apart, that picture the conventional William Craven, the first is a pencil and chalk drawing by the Count d'Orsay executed in 1843. Alfred Guillaume Gabriel, Count d'Orsay (1801–1852) was a charismatic figure: an outrageous dandy, a trendsetter, a man of wit, a shameless self-publicist, a sexual adventurer, a profligate and a gambler. He was also a moderately talented artist who became fashionable, sketching, painting and sculpting his way round English high society in the 1840s. The acme of his accomplishment, a portrait of the Duke of Wellington—the Iron Duke's own favourite image of himself—now hangs in London's National Portrait Gallery. Count d'Orsay also dashed off many sketches of eminent members of society with considerable facility, and in his portrait of the thirty-four year old Craven he depicts an exceedingly handsome but otherwise perfectly ordinary young man, dressed with conventional elegance, but lacking any discernable traits of character; d'Orsay was no Ingres.

A late portrait of Craven the conformist, dating from shortly before his untimely death in 1866, exists in two forms: as a carte-de-visite photograph and as an engraving taken from it. The stance and formal attire are identical, only the position of the arms differs in the two images, the lower arms and skirt of the frock coat having been drawn in on the plate by the engraver, Joseph Brown, who shares the credit for the print with Mayall, their signatures appearing respectively beneath Craven's left and right hands. By 1864, the carte-de-visite format—a photograph of approximately 3½x2 inches (87.5x53mm) [i] pasted on to a slightly larger card backing to provide a support and a border—had been popular for some five years. Individuals at all levels of society had their portraits printed up by the dozen for distribution to family and friends, while those of celebrities—the royal family, especially—sold by the tens of thousands. The secondary image of Craven that derived from the photographic sitting, the craftsmanlike engraving, was by this date an unusual by-product, photography having all but killed off the privately commissioned portrait engraving that had been popular in the previous decades. The photographic original was taken by, or at least at the studio of John Jabez Edwin Mayall.

Mayall's career followed precisely the trajectory of commercial portrait photography in its first quarter century, barely touching on the main creative forces in photography that occupied the 1850s, of which Craven was a part. Born in Lancashire in 1813, Mayall (originally Meal) later claimed to have learned the technique of the daguerreotype in 1840, shortly after the publication of the process.[ii] In 1842 Mayall emigrated to America and within a short time had opened a portrait studio in Philadelphia. His enterprise met with success and four years later he sold up and returned to England, to London, setting up in business first in the Strand, then in Regent Street, bordering on the prime residential area of Mayfair. He soon became one of the capital's most fashionable photographers, producing daguerreotype portraits that were commended in particular for their technical brilliance. A brief foray into 'art photography' using the daguerreotype proved unsuccessful; Mayall's clientele wanted attractive likenesses of themselves, not miniaturised tableaux illustrating passages from the poets. In 1860, by which date the silver-faced daguerreotype—each image hand-crafted and by the nature of the process, unique—had been almost universally replaced by the easily replicable photographic

William, 2nd Earl of Craven.
Engraving published 1st October 1864,
after a photograph by Mayall.

---

[i] The dimensions were determined by sectioning an 8x10 inch plate into eight parts and exposing each one separately by a system of shuttering, which naturally resulted in a much reduced cost per image.

[ii] The rise and fall of the daguerreotype, which prior to the invention of the carte-de-visite was the primary means of photographic portraiture for a decade and a half commencing 1841, will be described later.

12

print,[i] Mayall achieved a major coup when Queen Victoria and Albert Prince Consort granted him a sitting, which also included the royal children. The resulting set of fourteen portraits, in carte-de-visite format, caused a sensation in England and in America. The sale of images from the Royal Album, as Mayall called it, ran to some sixty-thousand sets, apart from pirated copies.[i] The carte-de-visite, which had been popularised in France the previous year, when Napoleon III had similarly allowed his image to be propagated, now became a universal craze—and the format for many millions of portraits in the following two decades.

Inevitably, the production-line process meant standardisation. Mayall's own studio, one of a rapidly increasing number in London, dealt with dozens of sitters a day. Most used unvarying camera set-ups, flat lighting that gave little modelling, rigid poses and often crudely painted backdrops—mimicking the backgrounds of the great portrait painters of the previous century. Also to hand was a variety of rather incongruous stage props, intended to lend a sense of gravitas to the male portrait, though the female portrait sometimes fared better, graced by the imaginative use of mirror reflections and similar devices of the boudoir. Typically, in this carte-de-visite image, Craven is seen leaning casually on a studio classical column, which has mercifully been removed from the engraved version, though leaving Craven looking even more discomforted. The piece of furled fabric leaning against the wall behind Craven gives the appearance of having been left there by accident. It is difficult to believe that a photographer as skilled and experienced as Mayall himself might have created quite such an inept image; it may be more charitably assumed that it was the work of one of a legion of assistants. By the very nature of the way it was produced, the carte-de-visite, particularly of the male sitter, was more-or-less limited to being a record of the subject, an existential affirmation. Yet, whilst the myriad carte-de-visite images have now assumed the kinds of values that attach to proven historical documents— being, as photographs, broadly a means of social observation; and particularly, by providing us with the sense of intimate contact with historical figures that only a visual description can provide (it is the photograph that makes Queen Victoria the most familiar personage of her era) the word 'art' does not readily spring to mind in describing them. Fortunately, we do not have to rely either on Count D'Orsay's facile pencil or Mayall's ready camera to penetrate the very private face of William Craven.

William, 2nd Earl of Craven. Carte-de-visite photograph by Mayall, 1864 or before.

---

[i] This is to ignore, as not relevant here, the ambrotype, a lacklustre process which in the 1850s and after provided a cheap and popular medium of portraiture, but which had neither the luminosity of the daguerreotype nor the convenience of the negative/positive system used for the carte-de-visite, from which multiple prints could be struck.

There are three known images of Craven dating from the 1830s, two surviving probably only as traces, photographic copies of the originals. The remaining image, a painting, is the earliest of the three. Nominally, it is the work of George Hayter (1792–1872), later Sir George, a fashionable society portraitist of the period (son of another, Charles Hayter, and brother of yet another, John Hayter) who was for a time court painter to Queen Victoria, on her accession to the throne, until Prince Albert took against him and found a substitute. Hayter was in all probability drawing master to William Craven and his siblings, and he portrayed other members of the Craven family in the 1830s, as did his brother, John. However, the 1831 portrait of the twenty-two year old William, 2nd Earl of Craven since the death of his father six years earlier, stands out as being unlike Hayter's other work. There is little stylistic connection between this rather unadorned portrait and Hayter's otherwise highly decorative mode of painting. In essence, the image is a self-portrait of the sitter. Craven used a compliant Hayter as his tool, much as he would later use a camera. He has required himself to be portrayed as a fashionably Byronic figure, a Romantic, a rebel against conformity. He is dressed in appropriate uniform for the part, voluminous black cloak drawn casually over an open-necked, broad-collared shirt and a dashing red coat; he has long windblown hair, and whiskers meeting under his chin to form a youthful beard. Such attention to the detail of his attire would be a feature of all his photographic self-representations, for Craven was fastidious. The backdrop to Hayter's portrait of Craven, the sea (Hayter's other portraits usually had interiors as background, or more stylised backdrops) tells of Craven's longing to explore yet more distant horizons—he had just returned from two years of foreign travels—as well as perhaps reminding of his father's daring exploits as a pioneering yachtsman, baiting French privateers in the English Channel—there is a sail on the horizon. In a second painting, of unknown authorship, Craven, some years on, still master of the image, projects a similar persona. This time his unruly hair is hidden under a peaked cap. The original of the final image is a chalk drawing: Craven, in profile, appears if anything yet more raffish, a tam-o'-shanter altogether failing to discipline the wild hair tumbling down over the generous side-whiskers that he will sport throughout his life, sometimes conjoining into a beard across his throat, whilst the mask of his face always remained shaved. The throat beard in combination with a clean-shaven chin is seen occasionally in other Victorian portraits; nevertheless, it was an eccentric affectation.

William, 2nd Earl of Craven, by Sir George Hayter, 1831.

William, 2nd Earl of Craven. Photograph (watermarked 1870) of an undated chalk drawing, c.1840s.

14

William Craven outside Ashdown House.
The first self-portrait, c.1851.

With his introduction to the art of photography, Craven took the portrayal of his image into his own hands. He did so in a manner guileless and honest, while at the same time more than a little egocentric. In the course of the 1850s, besides photographs of his family and his estates, Craven executed a series —or rather, what would evolve into a series—of photographic self-portraits that were objectively descriptive of himself, whilst being also intensely self-aware. There was Craven as the neophyte photographer, the country gentleman, one of a coterie of fishermen, a traveller dressed in the exotic habit of foreign lands; Craven as paterfamilias, the devoted husband, and—posed beside his gargantuan camera—as the man who finally wanted to be remembered for his photographic art, despite—or perhaps because of—having kept it hidden from public gaze at the time of its creation, in the 1850s, the decade that produced more photographers of stature than the rest of the nineteenth century combined.

15

William Craven, self-portrait as country squire,
in his suit of English broadcloth.

*William Craven, self-portrait as traveller, in a somewhat
eccentric ensemble of garments. The embroidered jacket is probably of Serbian origin.*

The future 1st Earl of Craven converses with Elizabeth, the 'Winter Queen'.
Detail of a painting attributed to Dirk van Deelen, c.1630.

History & Antiquities

At eleven o'clock precisely on the morning of 18th November 1925, the firm of Hobbs & Chambers of Faringdon, Berks, Auctioneers, began a four-day sale of the contents of Ashdown House, a faded, romantic-looking seventeenth century mansion built in the Dutch style of the period, but generally reminiscent of central European architecture, standing in a lonely setting high on the Berkshire Downs, some seventy miles to the west of London. As pretty as a doll's house, Ashdown still stands surrounded by the remains of formal gardens and what lies beyond them—seventeenth century woodland, a segment of what had once been a medieval deer park. A field close to the house is full of grey mottled, half-buried, lichen-covered sarsen stones, mysteriously resembling ossified sheep, survivors of an era long before the coming of man. After the sale the house was left in a state of near dereliction for more than thirty years. It was one of several houses that had belonged to a noble family, lords of tens of thousands of acres, now fallen on difficult times. This place, Ashdown, had once been the most favoured home of William, 2nd Earl of Craven, photographer.

Sir William Craven, Lord Mayor of London, founder of the dynasty (detail).

The origins of the nobility of the Craven family are documented in *The History and Antiquities of the Deanery of Craven in the County of York*, which recounts how the first William, born of poor parents, named after the parish of his birth, found his way to London late in the reign of Queen Elizabeth I and there made a vast fortune, being accounted one of the richest men in the kingdom. In 1611, Craven became Lord Mayor of London and was honoured with a knighthood. *In him*—we are told—*the commercial spirit of the family ended as it had begun.*[2] The next William, his eldest son, became a soldier, who distinguished himself in the service of the Prince of Orange, for which he was created Baron Craven of Hamstead Marshall, after the estate he acquired in Berkshire. Baron Craven subsequently dedicated himself to the cause of Elizabeth, sister of his king, the unfortunate Charles I. For the space of one winter, until her husband, Frederick, was defeated in battle, Elizabeth was Queen of Bohemia. Throughout the endless succession of wars driven by the religious differences between Catholic and Protestant that plagued Europe in the early seventeenth century, William Craven remained devoted to the so-called 'Winter Queen' and, when she finally returned to her native England, came to her rescue during the Civil War. Legend has it that it was in order to provide her with a last refuge that he undertook to build Ashdown, though she would die before its completion. It was this William,

19

soldier and romantic, who was created 1st Earl of Craven by Charles II, at the restoration of the monarchy. On Craven's death without male issue the title lapsed, but the barony and the title of Lord Craven passed by special remainder to his cousin William, thence by descent. The earldom was recreated in 1801 to reward the father of the present subject for faithful service as ADC to George III. Born the 18th July 1809,[i] William, 2nd Earl of Craven, photographer-to-be, inherited both titles and estates on the death of his father in 1825.

Beyond their names and dates of birth and death little is known of the lives of successive generations of the Lords Craven and their families, until the latter part of the eighteenth century—the generation of the photographer's grandparents. They produced soldiers and sailors, but neither entrepreneurs, nor statesmen, nor poets, and they lived lives circumscribed by the traditions and rituals of their class. According to the season, and whether they were hunting, shooting, fishing or hare coursing, they made their stately progress between the three main estates of Combe Abbey in Warwickshire[ii] (the family seat, purchased by the earstwhile Lord Mayor of London around 1611, or by his widow in 1622, according to differing accounts) Hamstead Marshall, and Ashdown. The Cravens naturally took a great interest in the Turf, the 6th Lord Craven being one of a hundred or so early members of the exclusive Jockey Club. The Craven Stakes, named for the family and initiated in 1771, was the first public race in which two-year-olds were allowed to compete, and the Craven Meeting remains to this day the opening of the flat season at Newmarket. The early summer social season passed off at the Cravens' London home, the last of successive addresses being at 16 Charles Street, Berkeley Square, Mayfair, where they entertained and from where they sallied forth to attend society balls. In the meantime, as was the custom, the administration of their estates, was left largely in the hands of land-agents and stewards.

The 1st Earl of Craven, ennobled by Charles II.

---

[i] Various dates are given for William's birthday. This one is taken from the baptismal register of St George's Church, Hanover Square, close to the Craven house at Charles Street. William was baptised at St George's on 6th August, 1809.
[ii] Originally Combe, as it will be referred to in this work, now always given as Coombe.

Notwithstanding the tradition established by their founding patriarch—William, Lord Mayor of London—of immortalising the family in paint, there is no great evidence of a Craven interest in art per se. The family accumulated paintings and engravings in considerable numbers, as was customary amongst the aristocracy, rather than actively collecting them for the artistic merit they might have. That is, the walls of their various establishments were covered with pictures but, other than portraits, they were ones that largely related to their sporting interests. Fulwar Craven, the 4th Baron, on his grey hunter, and Ashdown House are depicted in James Seymour's 1743 picture, *A Kill at Ashdown Park*, one of the earliest English paintings of the hunt. The Cravens were, of course, patrons of the fashionable portrait painters of the day, for whom they sat, and whom they often found unequal to the task in hand. None more so—as subject or as critic—than Elizabeth, Lady Craven, née Berkeley (of whom more below). She was immortalised by Sir Joshua Reynolds, whom she records without embarrassment as commenting that—*there is something so comical in the lady's face, that all my art cannot describe it;* Angelica Kauffmann—*it is a Hebe;* Romney, she thought—*has by no means given a just idea of either my face or figure;* Madame le Brun has given me—*an arm and hand out of all proportion to the chest and shoulders;* and so to Gainsborough, Beach, the sculptor Houdon, as well as several other lesser artists whose good fortune it was to have remained anonymous and therefore escape Elizabeth's vitriol, as well as by engravers and miniaturists.

Fulwar Craven,
the 4th Baron.

In 1826, Elizabeth, Lady Craven (1750–1828) wife of William, the 6th Lord Craven, youngest daughter of the 4th Earl of Berkeley and grandmother of the photographer, who, after her self-imposed exile and a lifetime of wanderings had settled for the warm climes of the Mediterranean, published her memoirs, only months after her grandson succeeded to the earldom. Elizabeth, then aged seventy-six, was described by a contemporary, in the home she had made in Naples, *working in her garden, spade in hand, in very coarse and singular attire, a dessicated, antiquated piece of mortality, remarkable for vivacity, realising the idea of a galvanised Egyptian mummy.*[3] The abiding image of the grand English dame in her sunset years.

James Seymour:
A Kill at Ashdown Park, 1743.

Elizabeth Berkeley had been married at sixteen and separated from her husband, on being given evidence of his adultery, thirteen years and seven children later. The terms of separation were bitter. He: *I am going to London; I shall not pass Christmas here; and when I go, I shall never see your face again .*[4] Yet in her pen portrait of him, written thirty-five years after his death, she shows an admirable degree of restraint, commendable so-seeming objectivity and, perhaps insulated by the passage of years, the ironic sense of humour that was characteristic of her:

His heart was naturally good; he had received what was called a polished education, though, perhaps, he had not cultivated his mind to the extent that the opportunities which he had might have afforded. His life was one continued ramble: to hunt in Leicestershire, to drive the Oxford stage-coach, to see a new play in London - to visit Lord Craven[i] at Coombe Abbey, or Admiral Craven at Benham, were his continual occupations. He had a dislike to remain longer than three weeks at a time at any place: which when I had observed, he kissed my hand, and replied - Till I lived with you, my love, I never stayed three Days in one place.

It is much to be lamented, that a man destined to be a rich peer of England should have neglected the talents with which nature had gifted him, and had not taken pains to form his mind or manners to that elevated situation. He was possessed of sound judgement and a clear understanding, but had neither taste for music nor the fine arts. He disliked reading anything but newspapers; and yet he never had a dispute with his wife.... (he) was at the same time generous and extravagent, and chose to settle all his accounts once a year.... The subject of the greatest uneasiness to me was the idea that (he) might dissipate his fine fortune, as he had it all within his power.... and when I represented to my husband the danger of living beyond his income, he offered to give me half his estates, and let me be the manager of the whole, allowing him a yearly stipend to throw away as he pleased.[5]

This offer came, of course, long before their separation, for Elizabeth continues:

Could I have seen or imagined that Lord Craven was as wilful and regardless of consequences as he really was, strange as such an arrangement may appear, I would willingly have consented to it (but) I constantly refused to participate in any such plan.[6]

Nor was the photographer's grandfather better suited to the cut and thrust of politics, though, as Elizabeth records, he did attend the House of Lords from time to time:

---

[i] His uncle, whom he succeeded.

Fox[i].... came to me one day.... and exclaimed, A miracle! A miracle!
I inquired what was the cause of his sudden surprise. Craven, he said, who
never ti ll yesterday opened his lips in the House of Lords, spoke. Indeed! I said.
What did he say? for he did not tell me on his return that he had spoken.
(Fox) then described to me, with much good humour, a speech that Lord
Sandwich had made.... asserting, as a fact, what was only his own invention.
Lord Craven rose, to the astonishment of the whole House. Loud murmurs
of disapprobation at Lord Sandwich's assertion had passed into a deep silence,
to give audience to a peer.... who had never before uttered a word. Lord Craven,
looking steadfastly at Lord Sandwich, exclaimed, - That's a lie! - and
immediately sat down again. The House burst out into a convulsion of laughter. [7]

The letters and memoirs of Elizabeth, Lady Craven contain far more than the tittle-tattle of a lady of
society of her time. Despite her protests—*Charles Fox almost quarrelled with me, because I was unwilling to*
interfere with politics a thing which I always said I detested, and considered as being out of the province of a woman [8] —
her writings are full of shrewdly observed character sketches of the great and the powerful, to whom
she was privy, and of psychologically penetrating analysis of their motivations and shortcomings, as
well as their virtues. Hardly more than a child when she married her fond, amiable, doting but
habitually errant husband, the fidelity of an eighteenth century nobleman being less notable in the
breach than in the observance, she began to find her own feet in her early twenties. According to
the scandal sheets she was apprehended by Lord Craven in a compromising situation with the French
ambassador; and it seems likely that later on, less publicly, she had other lovers, too. The historian of
the Jockey Club, Charles Piggott, a vicious scandalmonger if ever there was one—he would later be
incarcerated for seditious libel and die in prison—maintained that, *When Lord Craven perceived that she was*
become a democrat in love.... he was surly and indignant.... settled £1,500 a year on his spouse.... and advised her to
take herself off.[9] Surprisingly, if one is to believe the stories of Elizabeth's infidelities, Craven did not
seek to divorce her and maintained that he would not, just possibly because of his benign nature and

---

[i] Charles James Fox (1789–1806) the prominent Liberal statesman.

his love for her, more probably because he was much too involved in his own similar enterprises. For her part, Elizabeth remained married to him for fear that her children might be left penniless. But they would lead their separate lives until by his death they were definitively parted.

From her mid-twenties Elizabeth, Lady Craven, flowered as a writer of verse, songs, novels, travel books and, above all, of plays. Bilingual in English and French, Elizabeth progressed from capping verse—to his delight—with Horace Walpole, to the translation of a French comedy called *La Somnambule*. This appeared as *The Sleepwalker*, in a small edition printed by Walpole's Strawberry Hill Press. It was followed by a short novel excrutiatingly entitled *Modern Anecdotes of the Family of Kinkvervankotsdarssprakengotchdern: A Tale for Christmas*, which may have been original or may also have been a translation. In 1781, Elizabeth made her debut as a playwright and an actress. *The Miniature Picture*, received its first performance in her own drawing-room before an audience of friends, with herself, stagestruck since she saw her first play as a child of twelve, leading the cast. The play was then put on at Newbury town-hall, as a benefit for the poor, before transferring to the professional stage at Drury Lane where, the *Monthly Mirror* reported, it was, *acted for some nights to crowded and brilliant audiences, and received with great applause.*

Elizabeth Lady Craven
from a picture in the possession of
T. Floyd Esq. of the Hermitage, Newbury

Elizabeth Berkeley Craven as actress

The rules of the game being as they were—it was always the woman who had to bear the consequences of a failed marriage—Elizabeth was finally pressured by gossip about the state of her own—*Lord Craven, or his mistress, or both, filled the newspapers with the most unfounded falsehoods respecting me*[10] —and her purported liaisons, into leaving England. In the courts and grand salons of Europe, however, commencing with that of Marie Antoinette, she was met with no such libel or disapprobation. She was welcomed at Versailles not only as of right, because of her noble birth, but because she was beautiful, wise, talented, vivacious, good-humoured, stylish and witty.

It was probably in France, in 1783, that Elizabeth met the Margrave of Anspach (this being the first amongst his paragraph-long list of titles) the German prince who would become, in turn, her fraternal friend, her lover, her cohabitant, and finally, eighteen years after they first met, and with no regrets, her second husband. During the terminal illness of her first husband, Lord Craven, she had written to a friend, *I am told the Ogre is declining, but I can never believe it, because with his manner of living, he should have been dead long ago.*[11]

During the early (perhaps) platonic years of her friendship with the Margrave, as she travelled fearlessly across Western Europe and on to the rutted, wheel-busting, bandit-infested roads beyond, Elizabeth wrote him a series of letters that would be published in 1789 under the title *A Journey Through the Crimea to Constantinople.* It is worth mentioning that this redoubtable woman had reached the Crimea via Vienna, Cracow, Warsaw, St Petersburg and Moscow, in a voyage that lasted some two years. It was a path that the 2nd Earl of Craven would explore for himself almost half a century later, having become acquainted with his grandmother's accounts of her wanderings. Elizabeth wrote to a friend, *Notwithstanding the fatigue and inconvenience of the Journey I have taken, I am extremely glad to have seen the northern Courts.*[12] She received her warmest reception in the new royal city of St Petersburg, being feted by the aristocracy and received in private audience by Catherine the Great, Empress of Russia, who *treated me with the most unexampled attention.* In the latter part of the eighteenth century the Russian court and nobility looked very much to the West, and to England in particular, for its civilising influence, and the two ladies had much to discuss, including their mutual love of theatre. Like Elizabeth, Catherine was an amateur playwright.

Elizabeth's creativity is attested to by a voluminous literary output that covers half a century. But in her memoirs, whilst her opinions resonate mercilessly from the heights like the voice of Parnasus (Napoleon, for one, might have fared better had he been advised of her views on the futility of his Russian campaign) she also elaborates on the kinds of details that draw a picture of her upbringing at the most domestic of levels. Elizabeth has nothing but gratitude for the governess who oversees the first thirteen years of her life—before her own mother deigns to notice her—and who teaches her the skills and accomplishments that will be required for a life in society; but obliges her in addition to make her own bed, sweep her room and order the furniture. She is taught to manage her accounts in an economical manner. She learns elocution, dancing and French, but is also regularly made to visit the kitchens, the laundry and the cheese-farm, so being *instructed in another kind of knowledge, namely, housewifery.*[13] Later, in Poland, Elizabeth expresses admiration for the nobility, who take care to provide adequate pensions for retired servants. Yet, though of broadly liberal, humanistic views, Elizabeth was no revolutionary. She was born and remained the *grande dame, aux bouts des ongles*—the grand lady to her very fingertips, a description that would later be applied to the photographer's wife. Traditionalist and conservative, Elizabeth was of and for the *ancien régime,* as would be her grandson, William.

If we are to give any credence to the idea of hereditable factors contributing to the shaping of lives, then it is clear that the strongly creative predispositions that lay beneath the conventionalist exterior of William, 2nd Earl of Craven, photographer, as well as many of his other traits of character, sprang from the blood of his grandmother, Elizabeth. One of his grandsons would comment that, *He had a somewhat broader and more inquiring mind than the generality of his kind,*[14] and also that in physical appearance he favoured his grandmother. There can be no question of her having had any direct personal influence on him, though. During the latter days of Napoleon, Elizabeth was again travelling Europe, and shortly after his final exile she took up residence in Naples, where she spent the rest of her days. She saw little of her children, and their marriages and her grandchildren pass without mention in her memoirs. It is most unlikely that Elizabeth ever met the young William, though one is left wondering what sort of impression his grandmother's frank and intimate memoirs, published in 1826, might have made on the seventeen year old.

The photographer's father, William, 1st Earl of the second creation. Portrait by Sir Thomas Lawrence, c.1802.

The photographer's father was, by contrast, a thoroughgoing Craven. With his next brother Berkeley, he was schooled at Eton, *lodging with their tutor, who, like most pedants, was remiss in his instilments of the moral and religious principles which were to guide them through life.*[15] Elizabeth, disappointed that he failed in his filial duty to write to her in her exile, was perhaps unnecessarily austere in her judgement of her son, who would voluntarily give up his life of leisure to purchase a commission in the army—the conventional way for a young man to embark on a military career—fighting against the French in the Low Countries and in the West Indies, and being appointed a general (not a purchasable option) before becoming ADC to his sovereign. For this he was rewarded with elevation to the long-vacant title of Earl of Craven as the new 1st Earl, termed the 1st Earl of the second creation. Craven was a favourite of Queen Charlotte, wife of George III. Given her straight-laced views, he must have conveyed at least an impression of moral probity and respectability, though he most certainly raised eyebrows in the beau monde, in 1807, when he married beneath him, indeed, very much beneath him. His bride, Louisa Brunton, was an actress. The description 'actress' was not, however, in this case a euphemism. Louisa came of a respectable and respected stage family, being one of two actress daughters of a distinguished actor-manager, John Brunton. All the more unfortunate then, that the new First Earl of Craven is recorded by history mainly through the opening sentence of the memoirs of Harriette Wilson, the courtesan who purportedly drew the riposte from the Duke of Wellington when she threatened

26

him with exposure unless she was paid off, *publish and be damned*. Her so-called autobiography begins, *I shall not say why and how I became, at the age of fifteen, the mistress of the Earl of Craven*. It was hardly cricket. After all, the 1st Earl's mother had herself been courted at fifteen, and married at sixteen. Besides, when Harriet became his mistress Craven was as yet unmarried. Today she might just have been called his girlfriend and they would have happily appeared spooning together in the society columns of *Tatler* magazine, or *Harper's & Queen*.

The 2nd Earl of Craven inherited an estate that revolved around a traditional land-based economy that, by the early nineteenth century, was barely viable. The great surge of industrialisation that swept Britain in the second half of the eighteenth century was seized upon only by an enterprising section of the English landed aristocracy, those who like Lord Gower, owned tracts of land seamed with coal or other minerals essential to the industrial process; or his brother-in-law, the Duke of Bridgewater, who gained fabulous wealth through the operation of the private canal system, developed in the late eighteenth century to carry raw materials into the fast expanding manufacturing centres and industrial products away to the markets. A minority amongst this number became entrepreneurs on their own account; others leased their resources—including, for matrimonial purposes, their offspring—to the new industrialists. The new rich sought status by association, the old aristocracy needed money. Yet others, like the Portman family, which owned over two-hundred-and-fifty acres to the north of Mayfair used mainly for the dumping of London's night soil, were strategically placed to exploit the great urban expansion that began at this time. Many areas of London still bear the names of these aristocratic property developers: Cavendish, Holland, Lansdowne, Bedford, Grosvenor, and so on.

LOUISA COUNTESS CRAVEN.
*London Printed for La Belle Assemblée No 7.
by John Bell Southampton Street Strand Feb 1 1808.*

*Engraving of Craven's
mother Louisa.*

But like many of the remainder of the old aristocracy, the Cravens, who were no more than marginally involved in these various ways of exploiting their wealth, finally lacked, in Whitaker's phrase, *the commercial spirit*; or perhaps it was simply through disdain that they contrived to be almost completely bypassed by the material benefits that the Industrial Revolution and its spinoffs might have brought them. Whichever the case, it would have disastrous long-term consequences for their survival. The income from their estates, some still run on old-fashioned lines that favoured a free run for the hunt over the improvements to the economics of agriculture generated by enclosure, became increasingly inadequate to support their traditional lifestyle.

The family's wealth ebbed and flowed with the value of the agricultural land, which they continued to administer in a benignly paternalistic fashion. Bankers, with new business in their sights, would be increasingly reluctant to advance unlimited funds to successive generations of aristocrats on the security of land alone. The decline was gradual. From time to time there were upward blips in the graph's downward trend. But the final blow came with the introduction of death duties in 1893. For the Cravens, there would be the added misfortune of several untimely deaths in the family, adding successive waves of taxes. In 1923, Combe Abbey was put up to auction. The estate, of 6,952 acres, was divided into 166 lots, comprising dairy and stock farms, smallholdings, farmhouses, seventy cottages, shoots and fishing rights, a pub, and—as the sale particulars had it—*the Historical Mansion of Coombe Abbey with Beautiful Grounds and Gardens, standing in a well-timbered Deer Park, partly bounded by a magnificent Lake of 90 Acres with charming old world Terrace and Water Gardens.* Two years later the house itself was vandalised by the local businessman who bought it, *its carved oak staircase, panellings, moulded ceilings, Elizabethan and Jacobean carved oak overmantles, chimney pieces, Tudor roofing,* and all other removables stripped out and sold off piecemeal. The local newspaper, the Coventry Herald, *anticipated that... little more than the shell of a large part of the Abbey will remain.*[16] Two years later, Ashdown House, where the photographer's grandmother had begun her ill-fated married life and born her first two daughters, followed. It was emptied of its contents and left derelict in 1925.

The catalogue of the Ashdown house sale of 1925, which took place exactly a century after William Craven had made it his main residence, listed one-thousand-three-hundred-and-fifty-six lots, between them reflecting every aspect of life in a wealthy country house of the time and of times past, from copper kettles in the kitchen to Chippendale chairs in the dining room. But of the entire sale only a few items spoke of photography: *Lot 31. Large quantity photographic chemicals in stopper bottles. Lot 247. Enclosed photographer's print bath with tap. Lot 255. Full-plate camera in leather case, 6 chemical bottles in case and storage tube. Lot 256. Box and sundry photo frames.* Some of these items were discovered in the quarters of the family's resident chaplain, others in the schoolmaster's room. Of William Craven's own photographic activities no sign apparently remained. Yet it was here, at Ashdown, in the mid-1850s, that Craven's brief career as a photographer flowered and, with him, died.

As with his forebears, apart from his grandmother Elizabeth, little is known of the day-to-day life of William, 2nd Earl of Craven, except as reflected in the few surviving letters and travel diaries written by his wife, Emily Mary, the diaries of his wife's sister, Katharine (Kate) Countess of Clarendon, two brief and fragmentary family memoirs—and, as we shall see—his own photographs.

After Eton and Oxford, Craven spent a year-and-a-half (1829–30) not on the conventional Grand Tour of Europe that had long since been considered a proper part of any wealthy young man's education before settling down to marriage, but travelling a more adventurous and far-flung route, following in the footsteps of his grandmother, to Russia and Eastern Europe as well. His safe return to the main family home at Combe Abbey was marked by an echo of the good old days—a rather pompous little civic ceremony, and an endearingly earnest address by the mayor of Coventry, handsomely calligraphed on a parchment scroll and bearing the seal of the city.

To the Right Honorable William, Earl of Craven

May it Please Your Lordship
We the Mayor Bayliffs and Commonalty of the City of Coventry
in Council Assembled most respectfully beg leave to offer to Your
Lordship our warmest congratulations on the return of Your
Lordship from the Continent to Combe Abbey the venerable
seat of Your Lordships noble Ancestors

19 Day of October 1830 S Whitwell Mayor

Ashdown House, rear elevation, 1880s. Photograph attributed to William Craven's third son, Osbert.

The England to which Craven returned was an unhappy land. Despite its place as the first and greatest of industrialised nations, Britain was in the early days of an economic depression that would last for a generation. There would be no more songs of innocence. Conditions in the new factory towns reached a nadir, with the extensive use of child labour, unlimited hours of toil for the employed, and destitution and starvation for the unemployed. The laws of supply and demand, it was held, would control the labour market efficiently. Humanity was translated into so many economic units. To keep down the cost of labour it was necessary that there always be some degree of surplus, that is, a pool of unemployed; but the impoverished surplus then became an economic burden on the public purse, which in effect meant the ratepayers—the new middle classes—who resented the costs of maintaining these unproductive units. The New Poor Law would shortly be enacted to remove this burden, though not by bettering their lot. Those who did not work, could not work or, in the view of their betters, would not work, were incarcerated in the workhouses soon to be familiarised in Charles Dickens' *Oliver Twist*. A further benefit of the workhouses was to relieve decent society of the unpalatable sight of destitute workers dying on the streets.

Agricultural workers were no better off. Responding to the need to rationalise the use of agricultural land in order to feed a growing industrial population, successive parliamentary Acts of Enclosure had by 1830 completed the task, begun in earnest in the eighteenth century, of re-organising the English countryside from its previously fragmented and admittedly chaotic, but homely state. Small, scattered strips of open land, a survival of feudalism, were consolidated under great landowners; the gating of fields and the securing of their boundaries became a legal requirement; crop rotation was introduced. Inevitably, it was the poorest members of rural society who suffered, deprived of their traditional rights to graze cattle on open fields, and to take fuel from previously accessible woodlands.

Hamstead Marshall, 1850s/60s, photographed by Brookes of Newbury.

To make matters worse, in 1830, for the second year running, the harvest failed. Agricultural employment fell to a new low and already meagre wages were cut to the bone. Many families, unable even to afford bread, lived on the edge of starvation. Within a month of Craven's return, rioting broke out in Hampshire, Wiltshire, Dorset, Buckinghamshire and Berkshire—Craven's county. At Kintbury, barely two miles from Hamstead Marshall, where after two years absence Craven was visiting his mother, Louisa, rioters smashed up whatever new-fangled agricultural machinery they could lay hands on—labour-saving devices that were now depriving them of what little work remained and a particular object of their hatred. They then set about demanding money under threat from the landowners and others at random. Craven himself was held to ransom for the sum of ten pounds. Retribution was swift and terrible. Some three hundred special constables, raised from amongst the citizens of parishes from Newbury to Hungerford, joined by a detachment of the Grenadier Guards, arrested as many of the rioters as they could lay hands on. By the end of November order was restored. No one had benefited from the riots, least of all the rioters themselves. In the trials that took place early the following year, two dozen were condemned to the gallows (though all but one of the sentences was commuted) and dozens were sentenced to transportation for terms of up to ten years—effectively a life sentence. There was little chance of transportees returning home.

30

Craven had no part in the judicial process, but together with Col. Dundas and Captain Houblon, he had been at the head of the detachment of the Grenadier Guards that brought the rioters to book. Craven was without military rank, but the outrage to his person had taken place on his own home ground, and he was willing to guide the search for the miscreants. He had no political motive. It was the revenge of a young man of twenty-two, taken in the white heat of anger, and completely out of character with his actions in later life; for he was known as a landowner of the traditional kind, and showed the utmost concern for the health and wellbeing of the tenants and workers on his estates. His sister-in-law would eulogise him as, *the most unselfish of men*. And save for this one act of violence, it might be said, he was also the least aggresive.

Lady Emily Mary Craven, née Grimston. Detail of an engraving after a drawing by John Hayter.

In 1835, William Craven married Lady Emily Mary Grimston (1815–1901) the second daughter of the Earl of Verulam, and became in time the devoted father of nine adoring children, not an exceptionally large family by the standards of Victorian England. (In a letter to her mother that might surprise those who still cling to the image of the Victorians as taciturn about sexual matters, the youngest of the three Grimston girls, Mary Augusta,[i] wrote of her sister, the Countess of Clarendon, *what a hurry Clarendon is for Kate to be in a State again. I remember her saying that she should like to have twenty children*).[17]

Despite the anxieties of the Mayor and Corporation of Coventry, the Grand Tour marked, for Craven, the start of a lifelong involvement with continental Europe in which Paris, in particular, loomed large. Some time before 1835, the year of his marriage, Craven acquired an apartment at 9, rue de la Paix, in the fashionable centre of Paris,[18] where, later on, the couple would sometimes be found. Not all of the Cravens' travels are documented,[ii] but together they undertook several extended tours of the Continent, including in 1837 and 1845, and again in 1861–62, the details of these being recorded in travel diaries kept by Lady Emily Mary Craven, in the near-obsessive detail so typical of the

---

[i] The repetition of Mary is not an error. Craven's wife was Emily Mary, her youngest sister was Mary Augusta Frederica, wife of Jacob de Bouverie, Earl of Radnor, who was descended from the 1st Lord Folkestone.

[ii] Lady Clarendon's diary for Sunday 19th July 1863, for example, while on a visit to Germany, notes: *Clarendon started early in the morning for Wiesbaden - I and the girls dined quietly with the Cravens*. Earlier, she has mentioned their delight at visiting the Dresden Gallery of Art. No account of this journey survives in the remaining fragments of the Craven archives.

inquiring Victorian mind.[19] Alongside an almost encyclopaedic catalogue of churches, and paintings, on statues which, it must be said, Emily Mary comments with a keen eye and intelligent mind, she notes where they stayed, whom they met, sometimes what they ate, and always, of course, what the weather was like. References to her husband of a personal nature are rare, but illuminating. In her 1837 diary she notes with quiet satisfaction an occasion when her newly-acquired husband—whom she will always refer to as 'Craven', according to the manner of the times—brings their carriage to a halt at some point between the Reichenbach Falls and Grindlewald, and in a romantic gesture gathers a bouquet of wild alpine flowers to present to her. She would have been carrying their first child at the time. Writing to Kate later from Switzerland, she says that, *Craven is wonderful about getting up. I don't have to 'Come, Craven' him at all.* Whilst this might be an innocent observation on her husband's earlybird inclinations it seems at least as likely—recalling Mary Augusta's frankness—to be a coded message between competitive sisters on matters of a far more intimate nature.

If Craven's artistic flair came from his grandmother, his way of life was outwardly entirely the result of environment and tradition. His routine was bound by convention and class though unlike some of his forebears—views on fidelity in marriage having changed (at least, overtly) with the coming of Queen Victoria—he lived a blameless family life. Craven was thoroughly decent in his personal relationships; he was a declared Whig, a party best described as an alliance of patrician families who believed that the aristocracy ruled in trust for the common people.[i] He was liberal in his politics though he could hardly be described as politically active; he simply shouldered the responsibilities that he inherited along with his station in life—up to a point:

....boxes & similar knickknacks

> *I am afraid Craven's devotion to his duties in the House of Lords*
> *will not take him to London again today. He has been out hunting*
> *this morning.*[20]

In the words of a later family memoir Craven was, *a fine horseman and very good to hounds, a first rate all round shot, and an extraordinarily fine fly fisherman.*[21] He was unscholarly and laid claim to no very great intellectual pretensions, though, *a man of ideas, and impatient of the common groove.*[22] He was practical, quick of mind, and took a pride in the exercise of manual dexterity, in which he excelled. An accomplished craftsman, one of his descendants still has in his possession some of the exceptionally fine ornamental turned objects that Craven made—candlesticks, boxes and similar knick-knacks. Ashdown contained a dedicated lathe room which yielded, at the 1925 sale,

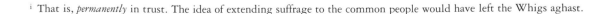

[i] That is, *permanently* in trust. The idea of extending suffrage to the common people would have left the Whigs aghast.

32

an ivory turning treadle lathe together with a very large quantity of beautifully made brass fitments, including gearing, chucks, and all other necessaries for doing work. The fitments are contained in a chest, mahogany nest of two drawers and seven other mahogany boxes. Like photography, turning was not considered an important enough accomplishment to warrant a mention in the obituary of a well-born gentleman, more of an eccentricity, perhaps, though one shared by quite a few of his equals. Craven was the owner of two of the Rolls-Royces of lathes, the Holtzapffels, numbers 1935 and 2103, having honed his skills on numbers 34, manufactured in 1789, 749 (1810) and 777 (1811) which his father had owned before him.[23] Father and son were instructed in the use of the lathes by a skilled craftsman provided under contract by Holzapffels, who would have been resident or semi-resident for the necessary period of instruction. We shall see this system of one-to-one instruction by a professional, then quite usual amongst the aristocracy, repeated later on when Craven takes up photography.

The young Craven also showed considerable interest in draftsmanship, and he left behind a folio of pencil sketches and watercolours, including a number of marine subjects, a youthful enthusiasm he would revisit in his collection of 1850s seascapes and ships by the French photographer, Gustave Le Gray.[i]

Behind the very private almost impenetrable facade lay a man of wide-ranging skills, who pursued his many interests with great seriousness. *The Handbook of Turning*, an important manual on the subject published in 1842, bears a dedication to the 2nd Earl of Craven; and so does one of the most important books on architecture of the whole Victorian period, William Eden Nesfield's *Specimens of Mediæval Architecture* (1862) which reads: *To the Right Honorable William Earl of Craven This work is respectfully dedicated by permission by his Lordship's humble and obliged servant William Eden Nesfield* (sic). Whilst a dedication of this kind may have been customary, Craven did earn the respect of those to whom he gave patronage. (The significance of the Nesfield dedication will appear later).

To say that Craven was a better manager of resources than most of his predecessors, or was prepared to abide by wiser councils, would be to understate the case to a degree. In 1809, despite the presence of French privateers who even after the Battle of Trafalgar remained an ever-present danger, Craven's father the 1st Earl resumed pleasure sailing—interrupted by the French wars—in the waters of the English Channel in his own lightly armed sloop, the 285-ton *Grafton*. In 1815, he celebrated the founding of the Royal Yacht Squadron, of which he was one of the original members, by graduating to a three-masted, full-rigged ship of 325 tons, something of the order of 150-ft. from stem to stern, and named *Louisa* for his wife.

---

[i] See appendix: Gustave Le Gray and *The Arrival of the Body of Admiral Bruat.*

Watercolour attrib. to William Craven, late 1820s.

A sketchy watercolour executed in 1824 by the fifteen-year-old William, signed with his own official title at the time (Viscount) Uffington, does scant justice to this imposing vessel. The successor to the *Louisa*, the *Mayfly*, which appeared on the register only in the year of his father's death, was a yet further indulgence. Without doubt, this was the kind of opulence that would lead to the youthful 2nd Earl inheriting, in 1825, at age sixteen, an estate encumbered by an astonishing £273,000 in accumulated mortgages—perhaps £15-million in today's value.[i] By dint of improved management, considerable belt-tightening on his own part, the sale of superflous estates, as well as—one may presume—the yacht (being uninterested in sailing) the young 2nd Earl of Craven—who claimed that when he reached his majority he had incurred no additional debts of his own—managed to allay the fearsome burden. By the 1830s he was able to resume a comfortable way of life, and to improve his estates, aided by the mid-century surge in the price of agricultural produce, without the introduction of new capital.

The 'Louisa' sketched by the 15-year old William Craven.

It would be idle to suppose that the entire world of the nineteenth century uncritically applauded the onward march of scientific realism, rationalism, materialism and godlessness, with the effects that these had on art and culture. Just as the gross materialism of the late twentieth century sparked off a search for alternative values, which manifested itself especially in the widespread influence of a quasi-mystical and half-digested mishmash of Eastern religious philosophies (whilst largely ignoring the inconvenience of observing their real spiritual disciplines) so, many people in the latter decades of the eighteenth century began a similar search for alternatives. Out of this quest (far more serious-minded than the latter-day orientalism of the twentieth century) emerged the movement known as Romanticism, which placed the importance of the senses, the passions of the individual, above ideas of reason and progress. Romanticism, in one or other form, would become a permanent fixture in the intellectual and artistic landscape, unlike the movement that it nurtured, known as the Gothic Revival, which lasted from the late eighteenth to the late nineteenth century, wielding a powerful influence across Europe over philosophy, politics, literature, the arts—fine and applied, and beyond—not

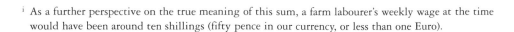

[i] As a further perspective on the true meaning of this sum, a farm labourer's weekly wage at the time would have been around ten shillings (fifty pence in our currency, or less than one Euro).

excluding photography. At an intellectual level, the Gothic Revival was the expression of a longing to return to the perceived values of medieval Christian society—the chivalric values of spiritual purity, piety, honesty, valour and loyalty, within communities no larger than might allow individuals to relate to one another harmoniously, and which enjoyed only the products of its own hand-crafted labour. In other words, it was root and branch a rejection of industrial society. And if, as one might suspect, it also promoted a somewhat roseate view of history, that did nothing to diminish its broad appeal. In practical terms, the movement manifested itself in many different guises. In a pre-industrial Germany long fragmented into small rival states, it came to be identified, most importantly, with the longing for national unity, and the realisation of a mystical dream of the German people to fulfill their destiny by asserting their leadership role in the world, and in doing so, recapturing their (mythical) heroic past—a notion which, divorced from its at-best dubious Christian message and paganised, would lead directly to the ideals that underpinned the Nazi horrors of the twentieth century. In an England which had no parallel crisis of identity, and was indeed striding confidently forward to what would be the zenith of its imperial and industrial might, the Gothic Revival developed no such sinister undertow. Its influence, albeit with moral messages attached, was most manifest in the forms of art, poetry and literature, and most enduringly and pervasively, in architecture.

On the 16th October 1834, the Houses of Lords and Commons were destroyed by fire. What replaced the gutted buildings, the new Palace of Westminster, completed in 1852, designed by Sir Charles Barry and Augustus Welby Pugin, was the architectural apogee of the Gothic Revival in Britain. The heart of London would soon be dotted with public buildings of similar persuasion, amongst them the fairytale fantasy spires of St Pancras Station, the Victoria and Albert Museum, the Museum of Natural History, the Law Courts, and the Albert Memorial. Churches, public and civic buildings and domestic architecture across the land followed suit. Humble cottages were embellished with windows in the shape of the Gothic arch. Grand country houses were refashioned to incorporate elements of the neo-Gothic, and new ones built according to its precepts.

Craven was not spiritually persuaded by the Gothic Revival in its renewed quest for the holy grail, nor by its intellectual mission, but he was certainly attracted by its secular expression. In the 1860s, he would add a major new wing to Combe Abbey in the style of the neo-Gothic, designed by one of its leading proponents, William Eden Nesfield, a student of Pugin (and a fellow Old Etonian, besides). *Specimens of Mediæval Architecture*, the book that Nesfield dedicated to his patron—with his approval—on his appointment to the Combe Abbey commission, is not only a highly important treatise on the subject, but in the design of the book is also in itself exemplary of the neo-Gothic style, as is Craven's unique photograph album, also believed to be designed by Nesfield.

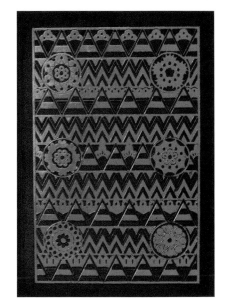

W. Eden Nesfield:
Specimens of Mediæval Architecture
(cover design)

36

Though on the face of it perhaps not fully compatible with other facets of his existence, the Gothic Revival seems to have played a significant role in Craven's adult life, including involvement, on one occasion, in an extraordinary piece of theatre, in which he became a player.

Amidst the high-flown ideals the Gothic Revival, in one of its more frivolous moments, also inspired the most bizarre public spectacle of the entire nineteenth century—the Eglinton Tournament. Devised by a Scottish peer of ancient lineage, Archibald William Montgomerie, 13th Earl of Eglinton, the tournament was the last rallying cry of the old aristocracy as power began to slip from its grasp. Since it has ever been the habit of the British to avoid doing anything precipitately or without due consideration, it would not be until the end of the twentieth century that serious consideration would be given to doing away entirely with the hereditary House of Lords. Nevertheless, the Reform Act of 1832, extending the vote to the middle classes, proclaimed the dawn of a new political era which would no longer favour the traditional aristocracy. Eglinton, born in 1812, and three years below William Craven at Eton, declared himself bored and disillusioned by the plodding era in which he lived, where, *all save dull reality is scoffed at, and imagination must confine herself to the everyday occurences of modern life.*[24] Eglinton's own inspiration, by contrast, was taken from his childhood readings of the exploits of King Arthur and the Knights of the Round Table, reinforced by the magic of the age of chivalry as it was recreated in *Ivanhoe* (1819) and *The Talisman* (1820) by Sir Walter Scott, the begetter of the epic historical novel, whose works would continue to influence and entertain generations to come, Hollywood film moguls not excluded.

As the ancient orders of chivalry were drawn from the ranks of the nobility, so Eglinton sought the candidates for his new Camelot exclusively from his fellow aristos, many his classmates at Eton. The Earl of Craven was duly recruited to serve. The full panoply of tournament was reconstructed in the grounds of Eglinton Castle, including the lists for jousting, a dais for the Queen of Love and Beauty, stands for the spectators, colourful pavilions for the knights and their retinues, and a monster pavilion of 120-metres length for celebratory banquets. No expense was spared, and Eglinton, renowned for his profligate abandon, would end up with a bill for £40,000—some twenty times the original budgetary estimate. Since the castle itself was large enough to house only the most honoured of guests, further accommodation was sought from neighbours of suitable standing in the surrounding countryside, or rented, or requisitioned. Meanwhile, in London, all of society began to prepare. Crowds of spectators gathered near St John's Wood barracks, where prospective candidates for the lists were at practice. Some of these valiants dropped by the wayside. Not as robustly built as their ancestors, there were those unable to bear the unaccustomed weight of full armour; others sustained injuries at practice; yet others were inclined to caution once they had seen the dangers entailed.

A group of the halberdiers of the Knight of the Griffin, William, Earl of Craven, take the lead; they are habited in the dress of the retainers of the noble family to which they are attached, the colours of which were scarlet, white, and gold; on their breasts is embroidered the crest of the Craven family; griffin statant, with wings elevated & endorsed of the last. The knight is on a warhorse which bore him gallantly in the lists, and which was equipped with the protective armour of the age. He, himself, wears a splendid suit of engraved Milanese armour of the time of Henry the Eighth, and of the best form & workmanship. It was a fine example of the skill & taste displayed by the Italian armourers of the sixteenth century and was purchased from the Marchese Tassoni D'Estense.

From: *The Eglinton Tournament, Views from Drawings made on the spot by James Henry Nixon, with Historical & Descriptive Notices by Rev. John Richardson.* 1843.

(The squire bearing the Earl of Craven's plumed helmet is his younger brother Frederick).

Those who persevered had to acquire the skills necessary to wield hitherto unfamiliar weaponry. For men brought up in the use of the epée, and the more robust on the cavalry sabre, the medieval lance and the two-handed sword were nigh unmanageable. Nor were their horses trained to this kind of combat, or to bearing armour. The Earl of Craven was reported to have done well in the field trials, and while the men battled on their fair ladies were equally busy educating themselves and their seamstresses in the finer points of medieval dress, whilst allowing themselves the necessary degree of latitude where they felt it appropriate. Lady Londonderry would attend one of the balls at the tourney elegantly attired in a dress of:

the early part of the fifteenth century; kirtle, with long sleeves nearly reaching the ground, and half of a costly brocaded satin and the other of a cloth of silver; vest, or bodice, half ermine and half cloth of silver, profusely ornamented with enormous diamonds; in the white satin lining of the sleeves, the family arms embroidered in gold and crimson silk Head-dress of diamonds and pearls.[25]

Eglinton Tournament: the lists

Whilst Lady Londonderry took a liberal view of the chronology of history, the noble Earl of Eglinton himself maintained a nice fastidiousness in one respect: the knights' armour had to be the genuine thing. According to the Rev. John Richardson's contemporary account, the Earl of Craven, under the pseudonym *Knight of the Griffin* (the griffin being an heraldic device on the family coat of arms, and the name of his father's first yacht) entered the lists wearing a suit of armour dating from the time of Henry VIII. A later, more fanciful account had him resplendent in a magnificent suit of armour which had last seen action in 1346, at the Battle of Crécy.

It was of Milanese steel, burnished blue, decorated with golden rivets and wrought in arabesque inlaid with gold. His helmet alone weighed forty pounds, and the bars of the visors were of solid gold. Many of the other knights had golden stirrups and spurs, but the Earl of Eglinton was his only rival in magnificence.[26]

For days before the start of the tournament, scheduled for Wednesday, 28th August 1839, the roads for miles around Eglinton Castle were jammed with crowds pouring in on foot and by coach, intent on watching this spectacle of medieval England. The fortunate, not to say adventurous few arrived at Eglinton by railway, on a line newly opened close by. An estimated 60,000 people were present when the introductory fanfare was sounded. Around lunchtime it started to rain, and by mid-afternoon the knights' proud plumes were looking sodden and crestfallen. The grand parade that had been weeks in the planning had to be curtailed, whilst the afternoons jousts got bogged down in mud.

Emily Mary, Countess of Craven, wife of William Craven. Engraving after a drawing by John Hayter, 1840.

The table leg, seen bottom left, is in the form of a griffin, symbol of the Craven family. On the right, the picture is framed by part of the lance wielded by Craven at the Eglinton Tournament the previous year. Attached by a ribbon to Emily Mary's left wrist, symbolising the bonds of marriage, is a miniature portrait of her husband.

40

Worse was to follow. The roof of the grand pavilion was found to be leaking, and the evening's festivities had to be hastily rearranged. The rain continued until Thursday lunchtime, making a resumption impossible that day. The crowds of commoners drifted away, damp and dispirited, though a banquet of sorts was held in the evening, somewhat reviving the flagging spirits of the gentry. Friday should have been the final day of the tournament, but Eglinton bravely announced an extension of the programme into Saturday to make up for time lost, and indeed, Friday turned out gloriously hot and sunny. Armour was burnished anew and the tilting got underway. Alas, much of it turned out to be rather less than thrilling, though the Earl of Craven acquitted himself with honour, having won his jousts.

Craven's sister, Louisa. Engraving after a drawing by John Hayter. The print is titled, 'The Belle of the Opera'.

The grand banquet and ball that followed that evening finally gave Lady Londonderry the opportunity to show off her finery to full advantage. But it was not enough to save the tournament. Saturday saw a further torrential downpour and Eglinton was obliged to acknowledge defeat. The tournament was brought to an end. As early as the thirteenth century a Castilian knight, Ramon Lull by name, then already looking back nostalgically on days of yore, had raised the lament, *Oh, you knights of England, where is the custom and usage of noble chivalry as it was in those days?* The knights and their ladies returned to London or to their castles. Craven returned south to his wife Emily Mary, who was six months pregnant with their third child. The multitudes of spectators began the long slog home along muddy lanes. The grouse, which had gained a brief respite at the start of the shooting season, sighed and resigned themselves to facing the massed guns once more.

Alongside Craven in the lists were two men, each of whom would become a source of family friction almost twenty years later. The first was Sir George Frederick Johnstone, a Scottish baronet shortly to be married to Craven's younger sister, Louisa Elizabeth Frederica. The second, who at one point in the tournament entertained crowds with a spectacular though unscheduled parting of company with his horse, was Prince Louis Napoleon, Emperor Napoleon III to be, but then living in comfortable exile in England. Photography, alas, was not present to record the events of the Eglinton Tournament. It was only nine days earlier that the formula for the daguerreotype had been revealed, with full instructions for its use, before the French Academy of Sciences. Camera exposures, it was estimated, would range from fifteen minutes upwards. Thus, the daguerreotype was incapable of enregistering a scene such as the tournament. Almost ten more years would elapse before the image of a large crowd appeared on a photographic plate.[i]

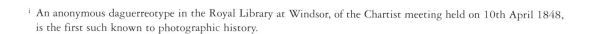

[i] An anonymous daguerreotype in the Royal Library at Windsor, of the Chartist meeting held on 10th April 1848, is the first such known to photographic history.

The Art of Photography

The unremitting growth of science and technology throughout the eighteenth century that was the basis of the Industrial Revolution stimulated a desire amongst the new middle classes created by the wealth of the revolution for rational and informed descriptions of their fast expanding world. The codification and wider dissemination of information arrived at by scientific observation was an important step in this process. Dictionaries, encyclopaedic and descriptive works on the sciences—chemistry, physics, natural history and medicine—proliferated, and new scientific journals began publication. In 1799, the Royal Institution of Great Britain was established for, *diffusing the knowledge, and.... application of science to the common purposes of life*, the very aims and objectives paraphrased in the Transactions of the Pickwick Club in the opening paragraphs of Charles Dickens' 1837 novel *The Pickwick Papers*, as, *the advancement of knowledge, and the diffusion of learning.*

Niépce & Daguerre portrayed in a prize medallion, 1902.

A notable example of the kind of effect that these laudable aims would bring about was the consequences of the inclusion in the first volume of the *Journal of the Royal Institution* (1802) of a report by Humphry Davy on attempts by Tom Wedgwood to obtain images from nature on a surface coated with light-sensitive silver salts. This followed on from an observation made seventy-five years earlier by Johann Heinrich Schultz (but pursued to no further useful conclusion in the intervening decades) that silver salts were darkened by the action of light—the fundamental discovery that would enable the invention of photography. At first publication the *Journal of the Royal Institution* had a circulation of less than one thousand. However, the report of the Wedgwood experiment was immediately reproduced in other journals and in other languages, and continued to be over the next two decades.[i] Despite the failure of Wedgwood's attempts at photography (because he was unable to prevent the images he obtained from fading) the reporting of the experiment—the first published account of an attempt to obtain photographic images—was a primer for the later successful experiments of LJM Daguerre, William Henry Fox Talbot, and a dozen or more other researchers, each of whom independently developed a more or less viable system of photography within the same approximate time frame. Science had at last turned the age-old dream of fixing transient images from nature—of suspending time—into a reality. The dream and reality were inextricably linked.

---

[i] In *The Photographic Art of William Henry Fox Talbot*, Schaaf gives 'a representative list' of fifteen subsequent republications of this paper.

42

Like Wedgwood before him, the French showman and inventor, LJM Daguerre, who had no scientific training but was possessed of a good measure of ingenuity, succeeded only in obtaining an image (on paper) without being able to fix it. Then, through the Parisian lens-makers Vincent and Charles Chevalier, Daguerre came in contact with an amateur scientist and fellow obsessive, Joseph-Nicéphore Niépce. In 1829, Daguerre entered into a partnership with Niépce to investigate a means of fixing the images received in the camera obscura. Niépce died in 1833, before the key discoveries were made that resulted in the perfection of a complete system of photography. Daguerre, however, persevered, and after years of making agonisingly slow progress by means of trial and error, he finally prevailed. In 1839, he went public.

The impetus that lay behind the invention of photography—the advance of a science-based view of the world—also propelled changes in painting. Inceasingly, from the mid-eighteenth century, but most momentously in the nineteenth, realism, as applied to the portrayal of the natural world, which had previously been an option of limited relevance excercised by a small minority of artists in the five hundred year history of Western painting, began to be widely recognised as a vital component of art. In France, this was at the expense of the dominant modes of neo-classicism and academic history painting; in England, of the fashionable, stylised portraits of the gentry, their horses and their hounds; Gainsborough's landscapes as landscapes bore scant resemblance to those he provided as backgrounds to his society portraits.

The Romans & the Sabines
Jacques Louis David, 1799.

In the vanguard of the new movement was the English landscape painter, John Constable. Together with JMW Turner and Richard Parkes Bonington, Constable would come to exert considerable influence on French painting—surely a close to unique event in the history of Anglo-French cultural relationships. With waspish humour, Constable sounded the death-knell for French neo-classical painting, commenting in a lecture on,

> *... the want of sense in David's large picture in which the Romans and the Sabines are about to join battle, stark naked, but with helmets on their heads, and shields and spears in their hands. 'What', he said, 'would be the impresssion of a spectator of such a scene...'*[27]

43

Constable's own painting was based upon the most scientifically rigorous observation of nature. He was a keen amateur meteorologist, who produced at least a hundred cloud studies fully documented as to time, place, and specific weather condition—*It will be difficult to name a class of landscape in which the sky is not the keynote*—yet his finished work was not science; it was art powerfully charged with sentiment for the countryside he loved:

> *.... painting with me is but another word for feeling and I associate my careless 'boyhood' with all that lies on the banks of the Stour; those scenes made me a painter, and I am grateful.... the sound of water escaping from mill-dams, etc., willows, old rotten planks, slimy posts and brickwork, I love such things.... As long as I do paint I shall never cease to paint such places. They have always been my delight.*[28]

In 1825, the French critic Amadée Pichot wrote:

> *It is not certainly without a feeling of mortification, that I thus proclaim the superiority of the English landscape painters over ours. I do not doubt that our artists will sooner or later feel convinced of the necessity of copying nature rather than models. To produce varied and powerful effects of perspective and light and shade, while at the same time due attention is paid to the minutest details, appears to be the secret of the English landscape painters.*[29]

Pichot's words lay close to being an unconscious prediction of photography. David Hockney has suggested that Constable used optical devices, including the camera obscura, in his cloud studies and other sketches.[30] There is no suggestion that this mechanical aid detracted from his art. Constable himself was clear about his motives:

> *In such an age as this, painting should be understood, not looked on with blind wonder, nor considered only as a poetic aspiration, but as a pursuit, legitimate, scientific and mechanical.*[31]

Constable was far from being an isolated example either of the use by painters of the camera obscura (the device that would shortly be adapted to use as the photographic camera) or of the change towards basing their work on first-hand observation of nature. Both practices began to take hold some considerable time before the invention of photography and had become widespread by the time photography was announced in 1839. For *The Times* of London to review a painting by John Glover, in 1821, as, *faithfully representing the scenery of nature.... to a degree of perfection which almost deceives the senses of the spectator*, did not require the invention of photography.

Yet to take literally the enthusiasm of the reviewer for what might sound suspiciously like late twentieth century photo-realist painting, implying an objectivity that is informed only by the artist's immediate point of view and skill in applying paint (somewhat analagous to the accusations of mechanicality soon to be thrown at photography) would be to mistake the meaning of 'realism'. To be moved by Constable's passionate depiction of his native landscape as seen in the light of the scientific accuracy of his observation; to register the geological precision of Caspar David Friedrich's rock strata in paintings that are suffused with mystical light; to observe the minute description of the structure of the natural world in pre-Raphaelite paintings whose subject matter is allegorical; to recognise that each of these, and more, have neither style nor intent in common, is to acknowledge that science and realism did not impair or inhibit art and its spiritual content, but contributed to it; it is to understand that realism cannot be characterised as a school of art or a kind of art, but is the lemma of a work in which the world objectively described participates as an essential component. Arguably, despite the sceptics, the same proposition might be said to hold true for photography as for painting.

In Paris, the public disclosure in the summer of 1839 of what would be called, after its inventor, the daguerreotype, was greeted with wonder, astonishment, and scenes of jubilation.[32] It was the greatest, certainly the most startling, invention in an age of inventions. With one bound, science had leap-frogged painters' attempts to incorporate reality in their art, and provided unimpeachable evidence of the objective existence of the world, without—for so it seemed—the need of a human intermediary:

> *Truly a victory - greater than any bloody one - had been won, a victory of science.*
> *The crowd was like an electric battery sending out a stream of sparks....*
> *In the kingdom of unending progress another frontier had fallen....*
> *the secret gradually unfolds itself, but for a long time still, the excited crowd*
> *mills to and fro under the arcades of the Institute.*[i]

---

[i] The *Institut de France*

45

In anticipation of the revelation of his process, Daguerre had shrewdly entered into an arrangement with Alphonse Giroux, a relative by marriage, for the manufacture of photographic outfits to be available for sale to the public.

> *An hour later, all the opticians shops were beseiged, but could not rake together*
> *enough instruments to satisfy the onrushing army of would-be daguerreotypists....*[33]

It was the mere idea of the daguerreotype—primed by months of press speculation—that had so excited the public imagination, for preliminary announcements of the process were already being made in January of that year of 1839. Yet before 19th August only a privileged few had seen the object itself, and even on the fateful day of the revelation not many in the seething audience got a close-up view of the real thing. The universal sense of wonderment that the first daguerreotype images induced in viewers can hardly be overestimated. What so dramatically differentiated the daguerreotype from any other medium (including other contemporaneously invented forms of photography) was its capacity for verisimilitude and its ability to record fine detail. Under a magnifying glass the image in a painting dissolves, whilst the daguerreotype—almost all of the early ones being architectural or topographical— reveals myriad details invisible to the naked eye. Yet, for at least some of those who did see it at first hand then or in the coming weeks and months, the daguerreotype was experienced not only as a triumph of science, but also of the irrational. Alas, no modern reproduction on the printed page—form with only a hint of the substance—can do justice to the physical presence of the object,[i] with its image as elusive as quicksilver seemingly residing on some indeterminable plane below the surface, suggesting access to hidden worlds within. The image appears both real and an apparition; reactions to it were commensurately complex. Paradoxically, the knowledge that the daguerreotype was a representation of places and objects whose existence and appearance was verifiable seemed to provide tangible evidence of the paranormal.

---

[i] Helmut Gernsheim's *The Origins of Photography* (1st English edn., 1982) attempted to recreate the sense of the daguerreotype by reproducing specimens in silver ink. It was a noble attempt, but alas the results do not sustain the book's claim that *the visual impact of the daguerreotype.... has been effectively conveyed.*

For many, at first sight, the daguerreotype had connotations with the Claude glass, a convex, usually darkened mirror, a so-called 'black' mirror, which was in fact not black but darkened by dying the glass in the mass, or by darkening the silvering in order to reduce its reflectivity.[i] The Claude glass was a device widely use by painters in the eighteenth and early nineteenth centuries, its primary employment being to contain and reflect a miniaturised, idealised view of a landscape, while reducing it to a single plane of focus, which rendered it more comprehensible to the artist: *In a.... convex mirrour, the image is less than the object, and hence the use of such mirrours in the art of painting where objects are to be represented less than the life.*[34] The effect of the darkening was to reduce the tonal, colour and contrast ranges of the reflected image so as to contain them within the limitations of the artist's palette. So successful was the device, that in the decades before the invention of photography its use became widespread amongst tourists, who might then pause before a particularly delectable scene and create their own instant, if transient view of picturesque perfection.[ii] With mysterious prescience, W. Mason, in *The English Garden*, linked the image with the future means of obtaining it, describing the Claude glass as *perhaps the best and most convenient substitute for a Camera Obscura.*[35] Prior experience of the Claude glass created a bridge to the daguerreotype, which was similar in scale, appearance, tonal range, and reflective surface to the tourist's convex mirror. It offered first-time viewers of the daguerreotype a momentary sense of familiarity with what they were seeing, though the experience was greatly enhanced by observing the extraordinary depth of detail recorded, and by the wholly unexpected notion that science had suceeded in fixing permanently this reflection of nature. In its first report on the daguerreotype in 1839 the *Magasin Pittoresque* gave the invention its guarded approval, while noting that, *the sun seems to be absent; one might well believe that the moon was in the heavens when it formed the mysterious drawing in the camera obscura.*[36] This description equally fits the characteristic image seen in the black mirror. A report in *Chambers' Edinburgh Journal* refers to a daguerreotype of an interior as *a mirrored sketch.*[37] In an account of a visit to Daguerre's studio in August 1839 to see the wondrous invention at first hand, Sir John Robison, secretary to the Royal Society of Edinburgh, describes a cityscape he was shown - *the appearance of* (which) *was that of the earliest dawn of day.*[38] And one other reviewer on first beholding a daguerreotype view in 1839, indeed described it as *nearly the same as that of views taken by reflection in a black mirror.*[39] The mirror, in particular the black mirror, whether of glass or of any other material with a reflective surface, also had a history in popular culture of associations with diabolism, sorcery, occultism and second sight, that reached back into antiquity.[40] It would be surprising indeed if many of those who saw the daguerreotype in 1839, two years before technical improvements made it viable as vehicle for popular

---

[i] Named after the seventeenth century French artist, Claude Lorrain, though probably in use before his time.

[ii] Convex mirrors are still widely employed today as car rearview mirrors and as security mirrors, for instance, in shops.

portraiture, did not arrive accompanied in addition by some of this familiar baggage of myth and magic, to ease the passage of science, just as, only twenty years earlier, Mary Shelley had used new science to *bestow animation upon lifeless matter* in her sensational novel, *Frankenstein*, in which the Daemon—a folkloric monster—is animated (galvanised) by the recently tamed powers of electricity.

Nevertheless, most early reports on the daguerreotype contained little to reflect the idea that it might have potential beyond the most prosaic of employments. Its role was predicted to be a subsidiary one: in surveying, in supplementing the artist's sketchbook, in making a permanent record of what might be seen through the lens of the microscope or the telescope; above all it would act as a labour-saving device:

> *To copy the millions and millions of hieroglyphics with which…. all the great*
> *monuments of Thebes, Memphis, etc., are covered, scores of years, and whole*
> *legions of painters would be required. One individual, with a Daguerreotype,*
> *would effect the labour in a very short space of time.*[41]

Details of the chemical process having remained secret prior to the communication of August 1839, none of the enthusiastic would-be users had any idea of the complexity of the operation that they would be called on to perform in order to produce the magical image—or the expense.

Making a daguerreotype entailed mounting a silver-plated copper plaque, cut to the required size, into a holder; bringing it to a fine, highly polished, unblemished surface and, in a dark chamber (part of the daguerreotype outfit) sensitising the surface by fuming it with iodine vapour, to form light-sensitive silver iodide. The plaque was then exposed in the camera, after which the latent (i.e. at that point invisible or near-invisible) image was developed by placing it in a further light-tight box and fuming it with heated mercury vapour, a highly toxic substance. Now fully visible, the image was fixed by washing with common salt in solution and subsequently with distilled water to remove the unexposed areas of emulsion.

By mid-October 1839, the daguerreotype was being demonstrated in public in London, again to the mystification of most of the audience. A reporter for the *Mirror of Literature, Amusement, and Instruction*[42] who attended one of these sessions at the Polytechnic Institute, Regent Street, complained that,

48

*The oral account of the proceedings comprised so many processes, and so many minutiæ,
that no one, without actually seeing the particular results, could remember what he had
heard, unless gifted with a most excellent memory.*

Months later, in February, 1840, another journal, the *Saturday Magazine* was still expressing the pious
hope that,

*as the subject becomes better understood, the process will be simplified, and placed within the
power of those who are now totally debarred from entering on a work, which makes
such extensive demands on their time and patience as the system of M. Daguerre.*

The hope remained unrealised. The operation of the daguerreotype was beyond simplification and
would soon be concentrated almost entirely in professional hands.

Daguerreotype apparatus.

In England, on the first announcement of the daguerreotype, there were no wild manifestations that
paralleled those of Paris. Here, a number of those with scientific interests appraised the daguerreotype
with coolness and sobriety before passing on to matters of greater moment, leaving the field free to the
entrepreneurs; for the French Government, which had acquired the invention from Daguerre in return
for public recognition and a pension, had then given it freely as a gift to the world, having made a prior
arrangement allowing Daguerre to sell the patent rights in England alone. The reasons for this
extraordinary piece of parsimony are obscure, but they certainly resulted in limiting the takeup of the
daguerreotype in England, as compared to France and the America. Neither was there, in
England, any sign of the daguerreomania that momentarily infected French intellectuals, artists and
above all, world travellers, delighted to discover a means of giving apparently more accurate and
realistic descriptions of rapidly expanding horizons than might otherwise be painstakingly delineated by
the artist's pencil. Within weeks of the appearance of the daguerreotype the publisher, N.P. Lerebours,
dispatched camera artists across France, the Mediterranean and the Near East to take views, but above
all to record the ruins of antiquity, some of which were subsequently reproduced as copperplate
engravings (there proved to be no satisfactory means of reproducing them directly[43]) published under
the title *Excursions Daguerriennes*. This early French enterprise stimulated no widespread Anglo-Saxon or
Celtic imitators. England and Scotland each produced only one single notable daguerreotyping
globetrotter - Dr Alexander John Ellis and Dr John Skene Keith, respectively.

It was perhaps fortunate for the future of photography that the general public had not been introduced to the invention via the portrait, for which it was in its early days widely lampooned. The natural inclination to Victorian middle-class rigidity was reinforced by the neckbrace or back-rest provided by the photographer to keep his subject still, and with an unblinking stare required of the subject during the extended exposure time, the daguerreotype portrait often conveyed an impression that can barely be said to fall under the rubric of realism, and can at best be described as unalluring. But within two years, with exposure times reduced from minutes to seconds, the daguerreotype was confirmed in its métier, and its continued employment would lie almost entirely in the commerce in formulaic portraits, overwhelmingly of the middle classes,[i] in which it became prolific. It was the long-term fate of the daguerreotype to become no more than a kind of bearer of mementos of family and friends. The poet Elizabeth Barrett Browning went to the heart of the reasons for its attraction:

> *It is not merely the likeness which is precious.... but the association, and the sense*
> *of nearness involved in the thing.... the fact of the very shadow of the person*
> *lying there fixed for ever! It is the very sanctification of portraits I think....*
> *I would rather have such a memorial of one I dearly loved, than the noblest*
> *Artist's work ever produced.*[44]

A rare early daguerreotype portrait by Vincent Chevalier, lensmaker to Daguerre. Chevalier, whose label is on the verso, died in 1841.

---

[i] Except in America, where competition was fierce and costs much lower, with the result that the daguerreotype quickly became a medium of popular culture. In his autobiographical reminiscences, John Werge, an English photographer, describes his visit to a 'portrait factory' on New York's Broadway, where people queued for daguerreotypes, four poses for a dollar, framed and glazed, turned out in minutes. See: John Werge, *The Evolution of Photography* (1890) pp.199–202. In America, the daguerreotype continued in popular use until c.1860. In France its decline began after 1850. In Great Britain its demise was rapid after the introduction of the cheaper ambrotype, a variant of the wet-collodion process (described below) in the early 1850s.

The picture of the 1840s in England and in France as perpetuated by the daguerreotype is highly partial. It is one of a social stratum, not a society. Images of the working classes were exceedingly rare,[i] not surprisingly, since the cost of a daguerreotype portrait in the capital cities was at least the equivalent of an ordinary urban working man's weekly wage.[45] The daguerreotype (or photography in any form) was of no more immediate relevance to the wretched poor of these two great countries in the 1840s than the early printed book had been to the illiterate peasants of the sixteenth century.

In England and France, the daguerreotyped world was peopled almost entirely by austere-looking men with high-collared, long, black frock-coats sometimes worn over brocaded waistcoats, necks adorned by soberly patterned cravats. The womenfolk looked, on the whole, somewhat more decorative— bonneted, lace-bedecked, and wearing voluminous dresses. In one of his numerous articles on photography, Charles Dickens somewhat sardonically describes the embellishments to one female subject's attire as,

> *of a savage style introduced lately into this country, consisting of a ragged tuft of streamers, knotted with Birmingham pearls nearly as large as coat buttons; a great deal of gauze, wonderfully snipped about and overlaid with divers patterns; with a border of thick white lilies round the cape.*

However, Dickens is seduced by this outlandish get-up when it is transformed by the daguerreotype:

> *Truly, a fine picture it is. The lady's dress suggests upon the plate as much delicate workmanship as would have given labour for a month to the most skilful of painters. The lilies that we did not like upon the cape, how exquisit they look here upon the picture!*[45]

Significantly, Dickens chooses not to comment on the subject's facial expression. Only luck or a rare degree of skill on the part of a photographer might enable him to capture anything approaching a natural look in a subject required to be totally immobile for the duration of a multi-second exposure.

---

[i] Thirty years of London photographic auction catalogues fail to reveal a single illustration of a daguerreotype portrait of an English or French urban working-class person predating 1848, other than a handful of studio genre studies. The George Eastman House collection has a very few portraits of street musicians and other such picturesque subjects. Of the toiling masses there is no sign.

While there is no hard evidence linking Craven with photography prior to 1850, there exists an intriguing possibility that, through a kinsman, he witnessed or might even have assisted at one of the earliest experiments in making daguerreotypes to take place in England, in the presence of Sir John Herschel, the great scientist and astronomer. In 1839, Herschel was recently returned from South Africa, where he had spent five years mapping the skies of the Southern hemisphere. He was living at Slough, not far distant from Eton College, of which his friend Dr Edward Craven Hawtrey (1789–1862) was headmaster. Earlier that year, on hearing the first reports of the new invention, Herschel, with his infinite intellectual curiosity, had set about devising his own system of photography, in which he was successful.

Dr Edward Craven Hawtrey (1789–1862) then just turned fifty, widely respected as a progressive educationalist, a linguist of exceptional talent and an innovator in many fields, had been an assistant-master at Eton during the time that William Craven was a pupil there. Hawtrey's mother was related on the Berkeley side to William Craven's grandmother, Elizabeth. Not unnaturally, the then assistant-master took a familial interest in his young kinsman's progress, encouraging and at once tacitly chiding the not overly academic twelve-year-old. In 1821, while on one of several sojourns in France, Hawtrey wrote home:

> *I had the pleasure to hear from my dear cousin some little time past, will you*
> *oblige me by giving him my love and tell him Monty is in the Rhetoric of Louis*
> *le Grand à Paris[i] which answers to the (5)th form at Eton, he is the 12th in*
> *Composition Latin and No. 10 in Greek in the school - about 400 boys.*[47]

Hawtrey kept in contact with many of his former pupils, and there is no reason to doubt that he and Craven sustained an amiable relationship long after Craven's schooldays. There would have been ample opportunity for them to meet, London and Ashdown House each being no more than a short journey from Eton. Hawtrey might reasonably have shared his own excitement with the new art of daguerreotypy with Craven, sowing the seeds of his later interest in photography. The evidence for Hawtrey's own early involvement comes from Herschel: Professor Schaaf quotes Herschel's diary notes of 1st October (1839): *Hawtrey Daguerreotype*, and the 4th: *Walked over to Eton called on Dr Hawtrey and saw his 1st trial of the Daguerreotype.*[48]

---

[i] The Rhetoric is the fifth year in a Jesuit school.

Even setting aside speculation about shared experiments with Hawtrey, it is inconceivable that Craven, with his extensive Paris connections, could have avoided becoming acquainted with the daguerreotype. But, like his upper-class English contemporaries almost without exception, he drew no special inspiration from it; in particular, one suspects, once it became primarily an article of commerce. Typically, curiosity satisfied, *Hawtrey appears to have flirted with the art only briefly*.[49]

As early as 1842, Sir David Brewster, the great Scottish scientist, polymath and advocate of photography, reflecting on the merits and demerits of the daguerreotype as well as the talbotype—or calotype [i] —the invention of William Henry Fox Talbot, questions the long-term viability of the former, while placing a caveat on the latter. Fox Talbot's system generates a negative from which any number of prints can be made. The daguerreotype, however, bears a unique positive image. There is no negative from which to make further copies. Attempts to multiply daguerreotype images by etching the originals and using them as printing plates are judged a failure. The metal is too soft to allow for long print runs without degradation of the image, and although the prints have a certain charm they capture neither the detail nor the sense of realism of the originals. An alternative application, using the daguerreotype as a base from which to create an engraving, as did Chamouin with his views of Paris, produced an image which retained none of the characteristics that so excited viewers in the original. Brewster concludes that:

Chamoin: Lac du Bois de Boulogne. Engraving after a daguerreotype. With clouds and human figures added by the engraver it becomes indistinguishable from any conventional picturesque engraving.

> *Our friends in Paris must not suppose that we have any intention of making*
> *the least deduction from the merits of M. Daguerre, or the beauty of his invention;*
> *which cannot be affected by the subsequent discovery of the Calotype by Mr. Talbot....*

---

[i] Fox Talbot first called his first process 'photogenic drawing'. He introduced the term 'calotype' in 1840 after advancing the process. See: Schaaf, *The Photographic Art of William Henry Fox Talbot*, and other accounts.

53

The great and unquestionable superiority of the Calotype pictures, however, is their power of multiplication. One Daguerreotype cannot be copied from another.... In the Calotype, on the contrary, we can take any number of pictures, within reasonable limits, from a negative.... The Daguerreotype may be considered as having nearly attained perfection, both in the quickness of its operations and in the minute perfection of its pictures; whereas the Calotype is yet in its infancy - ready to make a new advance when a proper paper, or other ground, has been discovered, and when such a change has been made in its chemical processes as shall yield a better colour, and a softer distribution of the colouring material.[50]

It was the lambent daguerreotype, not the photograph on paper with its graphic qualities, that had seized the imagination of the world in 1839, and began the revolution that the latter could not have created. In this sense, the daguerreotype has left behind it a potent legacy. But once the fundamental process of the daguerreotype was regularised it would quickly reach its limits as a medium for those with serious artistic ambitions not only because of the difficulties of manipulating the process, its high cost or its unrepeatability. Practical limitations as to size made the daguerreotype unsuitable for public exhibition. Equally important was a problem that Brewster identified as the *facility of examination*, that is, its highly polished, mirror-like surface. Unless surface colouring has been applied (which it frequently was, prettifying the subject at the expense of that luminosity of image that was the most essential quality of the daguerreotype, thus denying its essence) the elusive image can be seen at full-strength only by holding the daguerreotype at an angle to the eye's optical axis, so deflecting the mirror effect. And above all, in the daguerreotype the appearance of the image as it is finally presented is determined in a standardised chemical procedure, and at the point of exposure. In time, photographers using the alternative negative/positive processes began to discover, by contrast, how much of the artistic effect they sought to convey was to be discovered in controlling the negative before and after exposure—by selection of format and lens, by modification of the formula of the emulsion and the process of development; and by after-treatment of the negative (which we shall see practised both by Craven and his French colleague, Gustave Le Gray). Likewise, the manipulation of the print—its tonal range, contrast, density, colouration, surface, retouchability and even shape. These all become a natural part of the process of photography after 1848. To the photographer using the negative/positive process the relationship of negative to print is as subtle and comprehensive as is that of etching-plate to print to the artist. There is a consummation of intent in both that is unavailable in the

The daguerreotype image is seen at full strength only when viewed at an angle.

54

daguerreotype. *Thus,* in the succinct phrase of the great French portrait photographer, Nadar, *the daguerreotype gave way to photography.*[51] Seen in the original context, Nadar intended no irony. He was referring to the negative/positive system as photography.

Rushed into publication in 1839 in order to demonstrate priority of invention over the daguerreotype, Fox Talbot's negative/positive method was the only fully viable alternative system of photography; but it suffered from shortcomings, mechanical and human. The negative was made on ordinary writing paper sensitized to light by coating it with a solution of silver nitrate and potassium iodide. This solution impregnated the paper. The positive print was made on ordinary paper similarly impregnated. The resulting image, of an earthy beauty, appeared almost embedded in the paper. But this quality, together with the limited range of intermediate tones, gave the calotype a feeling much akin to more familiar graphic arts. It lacked the drama of the daguerreotype. First-time viewers in the 1840s often identified the calotype with the drawing, the etching, or the mezzotint. The calotype did not sell itself to the public as did its rival, for which there was no such comparable precedent. The realism, the miracle of minutely recorded detail, the ærial perspective (in painting—the employment of differential tone and contrast in a receding subject, usually a landscape) that Robert Hunt, the leading English writer on photography in the 1840s and '50s, called, *the magic of atmospheric effect*, that had sold an enthusiastic public on the daguerreotype, was not apparent in the calotype.

L to R: the sculptor, John Henning, A.H. Ritchie, and D. O. Hill. Calotype by David Octavius Hill & Robert Adamson, mid-1840s.

Furthermore, the negative/positive photography came close to being strangled at birth by its begetter, William Henry Fox Talbot, who jealously guarded the patent rights to his processes, effectively preventing their proliferation. Scotland was not then subject to English patent law, and there a small group of calotypists practised freely. In England, Talbot prohibited his invention from use by almost anyone but individually approved gentlemen amateurs.[i] Talbot himself took no photographs after the middle of the decade.[ii] The *Art Union Journal* of June, 1846, reported that, *photogenic drawings are not extensively known in proportion to the importance of the discovery.* In 1847, the first association of photographers, the Calotype Club, was convened. It had a mere dozen members (probably between a quarter and a half the total number of English practitioners) who were amateurs dedicated to the development of the negative/positive system, despite Fox Talbot's restrictive patents.

---

[i] Talbot did also grant a licence, for a fee, hedged about with restrictive conditions, to a very few commercial operators, besides which, John Werge in *The Evolution of Photography* implies that there were a small number of pirates, though he does not identify any of them.
[ii] Though he continued throughout his long life to experiment with new applications.

The Calotype Club of Edinburgh also had about a dozen members; and in France, Hippolyte Bayard, another of the independent inventors of a system of photography to emerge in 1839, was now using the calotype method, together with only a handful of his compatriots. Within ten years of its invention, photography had sunk to a very low ebb indeed.

It quickly became apparent to traditional artists that negative/positive photography was a far more reactive medium than the daguerreotype had proved to be. To many painters and critics, the daguerreotype's innate facility for the mechanically accurate but—as they saw it—artless reproduction of the real world, was disturbing. The daguerreotype was lauded for its realism and also condemned for it—it did not match the painter's perception of reality. John Ruskin, the most eminent art critic of the nineteenth century and an ardent advocate of realism in painting, who for a period made extensive use of the daguerreotype,[i] said that he found it beautiful, but never explained what quality of beauty it possessed that differed from that which he found in drawing. Finally, he distanced himself from the daguerreotype, declaring that it, *could never supercede art nor be an art in itself, for the simple reason that it was mechanical*.[52] (Ruskin would later, and to great effect, make extensive use of photographic copies of paintings—that is, paper prints—for teaching purposes). The ambivalence of Eugène Delacroix, the leading painter of the Romantic movement in France, on the subject of photography—the daguerreotype in particular—was typical. He made a servant of photography in the same way as did John Ruskin, and many other artists, using it as an extended form of sketching, a reference for drawing and painting—especially figure studies—whose chief virtue lay in the accuracy of its memory. But unlike Ruskin, Delacroix was also intrigued by some undefined possibilities of a creative nature that photography held out, as evidenced by his founder membership of the *Societé Héliographique*.[ii] Yet as late as 1853 he would write in his journal that, on showing a group of photographs to some friends after a dinner party,

---

[i] In Italy in 1845, Ruskin took daguerreotypes himself, and purchased and commissioned many others.
[ii] Formed in 1851, the first photographic society, and the model for the Photographic Society of London.

I made them try the experiment which I had made myself, without thinking of it, two days before: which is to say that after having examined these photographs of nude models, some of them poorly built, overdeveloped in places, and producing a rather disagreeable effect, I displayed some engravings by Marcantonio. We had a feeling of repulsion, almost of disgust, at their incorrectness, their mannerism and their lack of naturalness; and we felt these things despite the virtue of style: it is the only one to be admired in that artist, but we are not admiring it at the moment. As a matter of fact, let a man of genius make use of the daguerreotype as it is to be used, and he will raise himself to a height that we do not know.... Down to the present this machine-art has rendered us only a detestable service: it spoils the masterpieces for us, without completely satisfying us.[53]

At the heart of the problem was the last phrase of Delacroix's argument: that photography showed itself at once literal and unsubtle. Unable to fulfill whatever initial promise might have seemed to lie beyond its mere recording function, it had quickly demonstrated its limitations. Or so it appeared. Yet it could not be ignored, for it was literally made of light. It captured light effortlessly in a way that had eluded all but a very few painters in the course of five hundred years.

The hostility to photography was also part of a far more widespread fear, that a world dominated by mechanical science would strip art of its spirituality and bring about its death. Late in 1817, the painter Benjamin Robert Haydon threw a dinner party at his studio for his friends, the Romantic poets William Wordsworth and John Keats, and the essayist Charles Lamb. Towering in the background was Haydon's recently completed epic *Christ's Entry into Jerusalem*, into which he had introduced two observers: Voltaire, as the sceptic, and Isaac Newton, as the believer. Lamb protested. Haydon allowed that the interlopers were an anachronism, but held that they had a valid purpose in the painting. Lamb accepted the presence of Voltaire but expressed his doubts about the wisdom of including Newton in the role of believer since, he was, *a fellow who believed nothing unless it was as clear as the three sides of a triangle. And then*, Haydon observes, *he and Keats agreed he had destroyed all the poetry of the rainbow by reducing it to the prismatic colours.*[54] The dinner party guests were fairly inebriated by this time, but the point was made in all sobriety. The riposte is reflected in the lines of another poet of the same generation, George Crabbe, who had no fear of scientific progress, and used a scientifically accurate description of the behaviour of convection currents in his sequence *The Borough*, just as Constable used the same kind of measured observation in his paintings of clouds:

> *For heated thus, the warmer air ascends,*
> *And with the cooler in its fall contends*

Photography would be rescued from the doldrums under the impetus of technical innovations that offered far greater control over the medium and therefore held out a new creative promise. These changes made photography the medium of choice for a significant number of individuals who trained first as painters, but who saw the potential for science and technology to serve the ends of art (as did Constable and Crabbe in their respective fields of endeavour). Whilst rooted in the history of painting, these progressive spirits were ready to exchange painting for the new medium. With a declamatory flourish, Nadar described the 'Damascene conversion' of his contemporary, Gustave Le Gray, the seminal figure in French photography of the 1850s.

> *Gustave Le Gray was a painter brought up in the then celebrated studio where*
> *'Father Picot'[i] pursued the traditions - the last one to do so - of the school of David,*
> *Gérard and Girodet.... this school still maintained a powerful hold and hung on stubbornly,*
> *and Le Gray was uncomfortable with it. He found its rich diet unsatisfying and* (his)
> *restless spirit.... sought something more than its interminable marshmallow confection....*
> *As the young father of a family, he was enagaged in a ceaseless struggle between an obsessive*
> *need to be productive, the difficulties of making a living, and personal disappointments....*
> *He had always been attracted by chemistry, and painting did not cause him to abandon the*
> *laboratory beside his studio where he strove* (to discover) *the secrets of the formulae for*
> *permanent, immutable tones* (a quest which) *according to him, had been abandoned by the*
> *money-grubbing indifference of the tradesmen.... If there was one amongst us who was siezed by*
> *Niépce's marvellous discovery, it was him. Photography whistled. Le Gray rushed headlong towards*
> *it.... the die was cast.*[55]

---

[i] François-Edouard Picot (1786–1868) a neo-classical painter of history and genre scenes, pupil of David.

The Photography of William Craven

Craven is initiated into photography shortly after it has set out on its voyage of rediscovery, of revitalisation after having become creatively almost moribund within its first decade of being. The first of several improvements that would help bring about the renewal came not from England but from France, with the perfection by Gustave Le Gray of the waxed-paper process for negatives. (In England as in France, this invention was taken to have bypassed Talbot's patents, though he continued to fight a rearguard action for several more years). The translucency that obtained by applying wax to the paper before sensitization greatly improved the sharpness of the image and its rendition of fine detail, relative to the calotype.

Almost concurrent with Le Gray's waxed-paper process another Frenchman, Louis-Désirée Blanquart-Evrard, introduces the albumen print. In this process, which will become standard for the next forty years, the light sensitive emulsion, contained in a layer of egg-white, sits on the surface of the paper instead of impregnating it. The highly refined surface of the albumen print is capable of enregistering all of the information offered by the negative, it reduces printing time, and it extends the tonal range of the print—the last is what Brewster had looked for in his phrase, *a softer distribution of the colouring material*. But perhaps of even greater significance is that with the image sitting on the surface of the paper instead of being embedded in it the photographic print now acquires its own unambiguous identity; and whilst this is emphatically not a judgement on the aesthetics of the calotype process which in the hands of its most accomplished practitioners achieved the most exquisite qualities of tone and surface, it is an indication of the technical direction that photography is taking at the mid-century, which will inevitably modify its emerging aesthetic identity.

The complement to Blanquart-Evrard's albumen print is the realisation of Robert Hunt's prediction, made as early as 1841, regarding the employment of, *some transparent substances, as glass*, to carry the negative image. In the late 1840s several workers, in particular Le Gray, began to experiment with a newly invented substance called collodion, a transparent fluid made by dissolving gun-cotton in alcohol and ether. Laying to one side claims and counter-claims as to priority of invention, it fell to Frederick Scott Archer (1813–1857) a young English sculptor and experimenter in photography, to be the first to publish details in 1851, unfettered by patents, of the perfected wet-collodion process,[i] in which the transparent collodion acts as a bonding agent between the photographic emulsion and a glass plate substrate. The result of substituting glass for paper is again to provide for a yet sharper, more 'photographic' image, as well as shortening exposure times. The lifting, in 1845, of the heavy taxes on glass had the effect of increasing supply and reducing its cost by some eighty per cent over the next five years, making its use in photography economically viable.

All the processes described, with variations, would continue to co-exist throughout the 1850s, to produce arguably the most expansive and artistically fruitful decade in the history of photography. But it soon became clear that negative/positive photography (though not specifically by the wet-collodion process, still in its infancy) was in the dominant. 1851 saw the opening of the *Exhibition of the Works of Industry of All Nations*—the Great Exhibition—housed in the Crystal Palace, its purpose-built home of iron and glass in London's Hyde Park. Amongst the many delights it offered an eager public the world's first major show of photography: *never before was such a rich collection of photographic pictures brought together.*[56] Fifty-four selected exhibitors displayed a total of around seven hundred photographs. Discounting the thirteen American daguerreotypists (negative/positive photography was not practiced in America at that date) the European contingents were evenly divided between those who displayed daguerreotypes and those who displayed paper prints. Of daguerreotypes, even France displayed *but few,* and these were thought by the appointed jury to be inferior to the American ones; *but in her calotypes she stands unrivalled, and all but rejecting the processes of Daguerre, has concentrated all her energies in the further development of those of Talbot and his school.*[57] A sign of the times if a trifle jingoistic in the phrasing, and something of an irony since the British contribution was modest in the extreme.

The Great Exhibition, housed in the Crystal Palace.

Full of praise for the best of the photography on display, especially in respect of its technical excellence, the jury felt let down in one respect:

> *In closing our remarks on this department of the Exhibition, we may be permitted*
> *to record some degree of disappointment at the absence of specimens of the application*
> *of photography to any department of representations, other than such as please the eye*

---

[i] So called because the preparation had to be coated on to the glass plate while still wet, and processed after exposure before it dried out. This procedure which would not be superceded for some thirty years, was so cumbersome and time consuming, every photographer having to be his own chemist, that it had the effect of restricting the practice of photography to the well-heeled not to say dedicated amateur, or the professional.

60

or administer to personal feelings. As regards its application to an infinity of useful and instructive purposes, we have literally nothing!.... no specimens of copies of ancient inscriptions.... no representations of the microscopic products of nature, or the dissected parts of plants or animals.... no copies of pages of ancient manuscripts.... no delineations of tropical or remote scenery....[58]

This was virtually the same utilitarian list of objectives—treating photography as no more than a recording medium—that was advanced at the first public announcement of the daguerreotype in 1839. As to the last item, daguerreotypists had given them up more than half-a-decade since, and the glories of those on paper were yet to follow. Finally, so far as the future of photography was concerned, the jury at the Great Exhibition was still out, concluding that it, *holds a place at present intermediate between an art and a science, a position eminently favourable in either direction.*[59] As for the photographers themselves, if they remained reticent it was perhaps because there were as yet no theories of photography to propound, only practical problems to be grappled with. But fail or succeed, many of the photographers showing at the Great Exhibition were clear about using science to steer photography in the direction of art. In one of his lectures on painting John Constable had said that he aimed to show that painting was *scientific as well as poetic.* Photographers would soon be seeking to demonstrate that the converse proposition had equal merit.

A range of cameras was shown at the Great Exhibition but not illustrated in the Reports by the Juries. However, Chance & Co. exhibited flint glass 'for the construction of object glasses for Daguerreotype and Talbotype apparatus and cameras'.

John Constable's memoirs were first published in 1843, six years after his death, and four years after the introduction of photography. In many passages, conveying a feeling of nostalgic, bittersweet, romantic realism they provide—as did his paintings—unknowingly, the antitype for much of the photographic imagery of the 1850s, French and English; and provided a text, lucid and passionate, that photography itself lacked.

> *There has never been an age, however rude and uncultivated, in which the love of*
> *landscape has not in some way been manifested. And how could it be otherwise?*
> *for man is the sole intellectual inhabitant of one vast natural landscape.*[60]

The influence of Constable on the Barbizon school of painting, and subsequently the mutuality of the Barbizon school and the photography of landscape in the 1850s, has been well documented.

Contemporary accounts of painters of the first half of the nineteenth century encompass in addition such names as Delacroix, Géricault, Turner, Haydon, Palmer, Ruskin, Friedrich. Excepting Fox Talbot (the exception to most statements of a general nature) there is no equivalent literature pertaining to photography. Early photographic literature addresses itself almost entirely to technicalities. Unlike painters, we know next to nothing about the personal lives, thoughts, motivations or objectives of almost any of the first generations of photographers. There are no manifestos, no mission statements. Daguerre's own obsessive and mysterious quest lasted for almost twenty years. Whither? Why? How? The consideration of artistic aims in early writings on photography lies somewhere between the passing reference and the non-existent. There is no elevated debate on matters of aesthetic or moral values, for there is no prevailing ideology. There is neither orthodoxy nor challenge to an established order. To locate ourselves in the cultural ideas gripping society and being advanced with passion during the early years of photography—Realism, Romanticism, Gothic Revivalism (not only, of course, in the visual arts) we are obliged to turn to sources outside photography. For as with almost all other uses of the word 'art' in relation to photography in its early days, Robert Hunt's 'art' in his 1841 book, *A Popular Treatise on the Art of Photography*, refers to the exercise of skill and ingenuity, but unrelated to the production of aesthetic objects, as for example in his statement that photography, *now promises to be of important use to many of the arts of industry.*

There were those few who, even in the early days of the daguerreotype, when the talk was generally of its functional possibilities, who recognised photography's potential as a creative medium. And despite the later vapourings of the Ruskins, and the hysteria of the Baudelaires—*If photography is allowed to supplement art in some of its functions, it will soon have supplanted or corrupted it altogether .... its true duty.... is to be the servant of the sciences and arts - but the very humble servant, like printing or shorthand, which have neither created nor supplemented literature*[61] —there was little difficulty in recognising that photographs at their most refined level displayed all the qualities of art. But for lack of the kind of corroborative evidence that exists in relation to other art forms, it is only by seeking to penetrate the images created by the pioneers of photography (and to attempt to do so without foisting upon them our own anachronistic aesthetic theories) that we can begin to perceive what it is that they are describing and how, as well as to understand the peculiar qualities of the medium and how it began to develop its own aesthetic identity. There is no better way to comprehension than through what was in the 1840s and '50s of the utmost rarity, the autobiographical account, of which Craven's photographic opus is a magisterial examples.[i] In literature, autobiography begins with intent. In the pictorial arts it is the result of aggregation. The totality of Craven's photographic work addresses itself physically and emotionally to a self-enclosed world, a world bounded by home, family and social class; yet at the same time by the seemingly contradictory interest in modernity in the applied arts. It is defined by a quest for self-expression through photography. As we shall see, it also becomes, perforce, a dialogue with the darkness that threatens to engulf the author of the photographs.

Precisely when William Craven began to involve himself in the practice of photography remains a matter of conjecture, but it was certainly no later than 1850 or 1851, when he appears to have had significant contact with Frederick Scott Archer, inventor of the wet-collodion process. Archer was the odd-man-out of the Calotype Club, formed in 1847. In fact, it is not certain that he was officially a

---

[i] The photographs of Fox Talbot's kinsman, John Dillwyn Llewelyn, constitute possibly the only other significant example contemporary with Craven. Too small a fraction of Fox Talbot's (earlier) extensive output is autobiographical to be included under the same rubric.

member at all. Whilst the listed members were men of substance, successful professionals in a variety of occupations, or gentlemen, Archer was the self-educated orphan son of a provincial tradesman, who showed sufficient artistic promise to gain entrance to the Royal Academy Schools. After his studies he managed to establish himself, though somewhat precariously, as a sculptor. His work was not to everyone's taste. One of the many able though frankly limited and undistinguished sculptors of the time, Archer's figure of *Alfred the Great With the Book of Common Law*, exhibited in 1844, was savaged by the *Literary Gazette*, which described it as, *a tame, spiritless specimen of vulgarity*. Archer first became interested in photography possibly as a means of recording his sculpture, but it soon became all-embracing and he began to neglect his already precarious living in favour of experimentation in photographic chemistry. Like most of the pioneers of photography, Archer remains a rather shadowy figure. Gernsheim quotes from one source who recalled visiting Archer unannounced, in 1851, intent on learning about the wet-collodion method:

Frederick Scott Archer: Proserpine.

> *I met a thin, pale-faced, over thoughtful man, possessing a manner so free,*
> *unsuspicious and gentle, that in a few minutes all idea of my being an intruder*
> *was entirely removed.... he was profuse in description (as if I had paid him a fee)*
> *and ended with the words, 'Perhaps you would like to see me make a picture?'....*
> *But Mr. Archer's generosity did not end there. He wrote me a list of chemicals*
> *I was to procure, and told me to use his name at Horne & Thornthwaite's....*
> *He shook me by the hand as warmly as if I had been obliging him.*[62]

There is surely something missing in this picture of Archer as no more than a rather meek, self-effacing, Bob Cratchit-like refugee from a story by Dickens. In the first place, Archer must have carried a good deal of intellectual weight in order to be accepted by the Calotype Club, whose membership was of a high calibre. Then, while there is no evidence to suggest that Archer had any scientific training, it is clear that once accepted into the club, he applied himself assiduously to the study of photographic chemistry. Within a brief time, he had gained such mastery of the subject as would enable him, apparently without outside help, to bring to a successful conclusion the experiments then also being conducted by Gustave Le Gray and the English calotypist, Robert Bingham, in the use of collodion in photography.[i] The first application of collodion—a substance

---

[i] John Werge, in his autobiographical memoir *The Evolution of Photography* (1890) states that he has 'two collodion negatives made by Mr Archer in the autumn of 1848; and these dates are... vouched for by Mr Jabez Hogg... whereas I cannot find the trace even of a *suggestion* of the application of collodion... either by Gustave Le Gray or J R Bingham prior to 1849'.

discovered reputedly by accident only in the mid-1840s—had been as a medical dressing to protect open wounds over which it formed a hard protective shell.

Craven's collection of the works of his fellow photographers included two signed lots of Archer's, the first being an albumen print from a wet-collodion negative of a statue entitled (as inscribed on the mount) *Proserpine*. The light mottling on the background is printed through from the glass negative, suggesting a process as yet imperfect, or imperfectly controlled, that is, an experimental piece. The second is a group of six good albumen prints from unblemished wet-collodion negatives. The photographs are of the ruins of the Gothic Kenilworth Castle. These too are individually signed by Archer. Writing in her book *First Photographs* of an album in the collection of the Royal Photographic Society entitled *Photographic Views of Kenilworth*, Gail Buckland notes that it is inscribed: *The First set of Views taken by Scott Archer by his newly invented Collodion Process.... Ruins of Kenilworth, 1851.* Buckland herself dates the photographs to 1850 or 1851.[63] But why Kenilworth? And photographed for whom? Granted that since Sir Walter Scott's eponymous novel the castle had gained almost iconic status as a romantic ruin, are we then to believe that the impoverished Archer travelled over a hundred miles from home, bearing his cumbersome burden of equipment—camera, tripod, glass plates, box of chemicals, and some form of dark-tent for the preparation, coating and subsequent processing of his negatives—for no other reason than to take this set of photographs?

FIG. 32.

PORTABLE PHOTOGRAPHIC APPARATUS.

Frederick Scott Archer: Kenilworth.

65

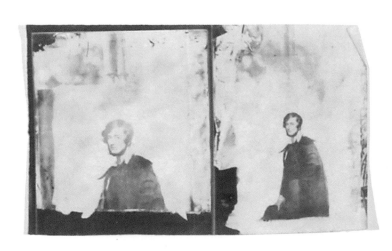

What suggests itself is that at the time he was also a guest at Combe Abbey, the Cravens' official family seat. Kenilworth Castle lies barely ten miles from Combe Abbey. It is more than possible that Craven was then being inducted into the mysteries of the wet-collodion process by Archer, and that in the early 1850s, if not before,[i] Craven commissioned some designs for decorative garden sculpture from Archer. The two virginally-new putti that feature in one of the several images of the parterre at Ashdown appear to be in an idiom reminiscent of Archer's *Proserpine*, and these were of a kind with others amongst the now-vanished items of statuary set about the gardens at Combe Abbey, where also, *the general array of vases, urns and cones* (were) *new and in Portland stone composition*[64] —the last being another recent product of Victorian ingenuity. Though the gardens at Combe Abbey would not be relaid until the early 1860s, the plans for the redesign of the gardens at Ashdown were drawn up a decade earlier, and the work completed within the lifetime of Archer.

Seven small-scale untrimmed albumen prints of irregular sizes, discovered in a brown paper envelope, are all that remain of what was doubtless one of Craven's earliest attempts at photography. Six of the seven are copies of paintings. The last is a pale print[ii] of a male figure leaning against the stone balustrade at Ashdown, that appears in the background to several later images. The figure is unidentified, but though he is bearded, the powerful nose, heavy brow and deep forehead are strongly suggestive of a clean-shaven Scott Archer, as he appears in a portrait taken some five or six years later. What could be more obvious than that the master stand in as his pupil's model? The other six prints, grouped two and four, are of the two previously mentioned photographic copies of paintings of Craven as a dandyish, Byronic young man, the one by George Hayter, dated 1831, plus the later unattributed one. The copies of the paintings each have the background of the original blocked-out by retouching the photographic negative, isolating and emphasizing the central figure. These may have been a practise run for this device, which Craven would employ again later on to good effect.

Digitally enhanced detail of top right image on facing page.

FREDERICK SCOTT ARCHER.

Frederick Scott Archer, 1855.

---

[i] The banded rustication to the (image) left of *Proserpine* appears to show that the photograph was taken against the same background as Craven's first self-portrait.

[ii] Either because the negative was under-exposed and was therefore not capable of being printed to a full depth of tone, or because the positive was not fully printed-out.

The earliest image to have emerged from the folios proper, one that is by turns revelatory and enigmatic, is a full-length study of Craven himself. The surviving print is torn and distressed. Craven is found standing outside one of the single-storey buildings—stables and staff quarters—that flank the frontage of Ashdown House. These outbuildings have been remodelled since, and it is not possible to pinpoint the precise location of the photograph. However, a detail of a companion pair of wide views of the rear of the house taken somewhat later reveals in the visible part of one of the outbuildings a circular window similar to the one partially visible at the top lefthand corner of the full-length portrait. And the banded rustication—the horizontal detailing on the stonework visible behind Craven's right shoulder—is featured repeatedly with variations on the house itself, as well as on the outbuildings.

Craven's gesture idicates that he is left-handed, and that this is a self-portrait (meaning, one conceived and set up by the subject, though in execution it would of course have required the aid of an assistant to draw out the dark-slide and uncap the lens for the exposure to take place). The gesture is deliberate: the fingers of the left hand are curling upwards against the thumb in such a manner as to suggest that Craven is counting off the seconds-long exposure. That is, he is identifying himself in fact as the photographer.[i] The self-description of the artist in the act of painting, or associated with symbols that identify the subject as an artist is, like the self-portrait itself, a piece of iconography going back at least to the pre-renaissance period, of which there are a multitude of examples, ranging from Roger Van Der Weyden's depiction of himself as St Luke (the patron saint of painters in the Middle Ages) painting the Virgin and Child, or Grunewald's slightly later self-portrait holding a pen or burin; to Gainsborough, Reynolds and Elisabeth-Louise Vigée Le Brun—the successful society portraitist who was the object of Craven's grandmother's sarcastic assessment—holding her palette and brush.[65] Le Brun died in 1842, by which time photographers had already embraced the idea of the self-portrait.

An analysis of what we observe in the print will tell us a good deal about Craven's beginnings in photography.

---

[i] Photographers' self-portraits would often feature a camera in shot. Here presumably there was no second camera to hand.

There are four layers involved in the making of the print: the topmost is a sheet of glass, which has been used to retain the negative—the second layer—securely in position on the third layer, the printing paper. The fourth, bottom layer, generally a board covered with velvet, baize, or a similar material, acts as a smooth, flat support for the layers above it. The entire arrangement would usually have been secured within a wooden frame. But Sparling allows that the bottom layer might be *simple squares of glass…. (and the whole) held together by the wooden clips sold at the American warehouses at one shilling per dozen.*[66]

Since here the image of the edge of the topmost glass is visible near the lower and right edges of the print, and the printed image continues beyond the boundaries of the glass, it is evident that this glass is not the negative itself, but a cover-glass positioned somewhat carelessly and without the security of the wooden clips.

The soft, dense quality of the image, as well as two creases across the bottom right corner—which have printed through from the negative as whitish lines—indicates that the negative is a paper one, that is, a calotype. Whilst the negative may have been in existence for some time before the print was made, the print itself is albumenised, and therefore cannot predate 1850/1. This tallies with what we are able to observe from the cover glass: it has been used previously to make a collodion negative, which presumably turned out unsatisfactory in some way, so the emulsion has been stripped off in order that the glass might be reused. Glass was an expensive commodity, and this was common practice. The stripping has not been carried out very effectively, and has left behind two clues as to prior use. First, there are dart-shaped marks or 'comets' present, of which the most prominent is to be seen just above the centre of Craven's coat. All photographic manuals of the wet-collodion period point to the extreme care that has to be taken in cleaning the glass plate preparatory to coating, and then in applying the layer of collodion by pouring it on to the glass, which is held at a slight angle to the horizontal. Towler's *The Silver Sunbeam* [67] points to one of the dangers of preparing too much collodion for immediate use, and recorking the residue: *Collodion is apt to indurate around the orifice of the bottle; and if this dry film is not carefully removed every time, it may cause trouble by flowing off in fragments along with the collodion.* These fragments then become islands embedded in the layer of collodion around which the light sensitive emulsion, applied subsequently, coagulates, forming the characteristic comets seen here.[i] When enlarged, the white mark (on the print) at the lower right corner of the cover glass can clearly be seen to be a fingerprint. Various devices for handling sheets of glass without touching the surface were developed over the next few years, but this continued to be a problem in the case of Craven's large format negatives.

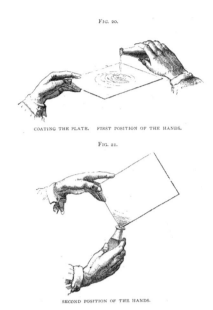

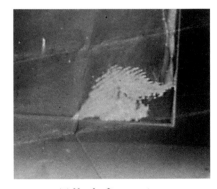

Telltale fingerprint.
(digitally enhanced image)

The second clue lies in the vertical white line in the middle of the doorway and the white marks on the doorpost and elsewhere, caused by fragments of collodion and emulsion that have remained attached to the glass. To reinforce the point, it may be noted that there is no debris from the collodion process in the image area outside the imprint of the cover glass. From this print we are able to conclude, then, that Craven tried both the calotype and wet-collodion processes before opting for the latter; that he may have commenced taking photographs in the pre-collodion period, that is before 1850 (with or without the help of Archer) but not by much, given the unusually large size of the negative for that time (approximately 13x10 inches, 33x25cm.). And finally, since it hardly seems likely that Craven used the calotype process to make only the one single self-portrait, it must be concluded that a whole tranche of his early work has, alas, been lost.

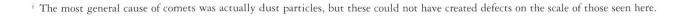

[i] The most general cause of comets was actually dust particles, but these could not have created defects on the scale of those seen here.

The grand opening of the photographic exhibition at the Society of Arts.

72

After the encounter with Archer, Craven, on the threshold of photography, becomes virtually invisible until some time in 1853. In old age his second daughter, Evelyn Mary, replayed a vivid memory of the family travelling to London in September, 1852, to attend the funeral of the Duke of Wellington. The London-bound train stops at Shrivenham, the Craven state coach and draft-horses are taken on board, and off they go. It is an isolated anecdote. There are no known letters extant from Emily Mary to her sister Kate in this period, and by unfortunate coincidence no diaries of Kate's between early 1851 and December, 1853; these must be presumed lost. More puzzlingly, there are no Craven photographs that can be located between the first self-portrait and 1853. Did Craven continue to practise photography in the interim? Did he perhaps destroy the work of his early years because he found it lacking? If so, or if he had simply failed for whatever reasons to pursue his initial interest, it was certainly rekindled by the exhibition of photographs hosted by the Society of Arts, that opened with a grand soirée in December 1852. Significantly, the *Illustrated London News* reported that, *the exhibition has been confined to productions on paper and on glass, to the entire exclusion of Daguerréotypes*. At the soirée, Roger Fenton—the leading advocate for the establishment of a photographic society—read a paper *On the present Position and future Prospects of the art of Photography*. The latter had been given a major fillip by Talbot's recent relaxation— under extreme pressure—of his restrictive patents.

The Photographic Society was duly called into being on 20th January 1853. It received Royal approval. Queen Victoria and Prince Albert were both keen on photography and took instruction in it, and it would in due course be retitled the Royal Photographic Society.

William Craven comes across as an intensely private individual. He did not join the Photographic Society immediately, though he would do so the following year, and thereafter remain a member for the rest of his life. His reservations about maintaining his privacy, however, constrained any ambitions he might have harboured about exhibiting his photographs. Or might it have been a lack of self-confidence? Most photographers of the period saw themselves as a band of brothers, vying with one another in open competition, and squabbling with one another in print over chemical formulae. But Craven risked exposure on the walls of a gallery only two occasions, and then he showed works that can best be described, in all charity, as unrepresentative of his highest achievements.

A Vase of Ferns.

Two prints that Craven submitted were selected for the second annual exhibition of the Photographic Society, held in January 1855. The information is more interesting for the record than it is of help in tracking the Craven chronology, since neither of the entries—taken some while after the commencement of his most active period as a photographer—can now be identified with certainty. The one listed as *no. 12* was simply entitled *From Life*. It may well have been another print of *A Vase of Ferns*, the only still-life found in the Craven folios.[i] The alternative, of extant images, would be one of the compositions of dead game birds—of which there are several examples in the folios—if these may without too great an irony be described as *'from life'*. The *Vase of Ferns* and the best of the game birds, *A Brace and a Half of Partridges*, both appear in the folios and again in the great album, indicating at least that Craven still retained some regard for these images when he looked on them again years later.

A Brace and a Half of Partridges.

---

[i] The print found in the folio was unmounted. The one exhibited would have been mounted.

The other print shown at the Photographic Society was listed as *no. 57, Ashdown House, the Seat of the Earl of Craven*. However, the only known extant view of Ashdown House not accounted for in the tally of views taken in 1855 (to be detailed later in context) is one of the front of the house seen in winter. Set against the powerfully realised vision of subsequent images of the house this appears a somewhat tentative composition, at best. If this was indeed *no. 57*, it can have gained Craven small merit. And unlike the richly sepia *Vase of Ferns* and *Brace and a Half of Partridges* the surviving print of the house is of a pallid, indeterminate colouration and lacks tonality. It has certainly not been treated with the gold chloride bath that is surely the process that gives so many of Craven's other prints their enduring richness of tone.

1856 saw the publication of an extensive photographic manual written by Marcus Sparling, recently returned from the Crimea where he had been assistant to Roger Fenton in photographing the war (see below). In this manual, which was particularly detailed in the area of photographic chemistry, Sparling noted in respect of chloride of gold that, *its chief use in photography is the property it possesses of blackening the shadows of a positive print, which it does to a wonderful extent*.[68] This quality, which Craven developed to a fine art, would be characteristic of the best of his œvre with the general exception of his portraits. Sparling continues by quoting Thomas Sutton's full description of the process, which had peviously been *communicated to the Photographic Journal in the month of March, 1855*. Sutton says: *by removing the print before the deposit of gold has fully taken place, you obtain a dark red-purple print, and by a longer action a violet-purple approaching to black*.[69] Apart from dictating the hue and intensity of the print, the gold chloride bath provided a further and highly important benefit. Gold is one of the most stable elements known and its application in this context, where it substitutes for part of the silver content in the emulsion, makes the print resistant to fading.[i]

Ashdown House,
the Seat of the Earl of Craven

---

[i] Toning with platinum and with selenium, each of which shares the virtue of stability with gold whilst endowing the print its own pictorial characteristics, would later be added to the photographer's armoury. Like all photographers of the period Craven's prints were variable as to colour, density, contrast and tonality. This would not necessarily have been by intent alone, but might equally have been the result of using chemicals of unreliable quality, along with the problems of maintaining solutions at a constant temperature and the intensity and colour temperature of the daylight that was the only light source for printing, and which varies according to time of day, sky/cloud conditions, and time of year.

Craven exhibited for the second and probably last time In 1856,[i] at the Photographic Society of Scotland, possibly at the suggestion of Roger Fenton, who also showed at this exhibition. The image was far more unusual and arresting than those of the previous year. Its subject was *Wild Darrell, Winner of the Derby, 1855*.[70] After the race Craven had given one of his daughters, Evelyn Mary, a locket containing a wisp of the horse's mane with the name on it spelled thus, though it appears as *Wild Dayrell*—his correct given name—in Taunton's *Portraits of Celebrated Racehorses*,[71] as well as in studbooks and other histories of the Turf. The naming of the colt as Wild Darrell appears to have been, as we shall see, a somewhat macabre joke concocted by the Cravens and their neighbour, Francis L Popham, Esq., of Littlecote Park.

Popham first ventured into horse breeding in 1850, when he purchased Wild Darrell's dam for £50, together with another thoroughbred mare. Both mares went to a stallion in 1851, and Wild Darrell and his half-sister were born in 1852, but as Popham had no trainer to put them to work he decided to offer both foals at auction. The yearlings showed great promise and Popham made a substantial profit on the sale. Within a year, Popham regretted his hasty decision and repurchased them; enter the Earl of Craven. According to family tradition, Popham was short of ready cash at the time and Craven obliged him by buying a part share in Wild Darrell. Craven avoided being publicly associated with ownership of the horse; Taunton's *Portraits* mentions only Popham. The reasons for this are not explained, but it was either a further example of Craven being shy of publicity, or equally likely, though the Cravens themselves were certainly not snobs, it related to the unyielding nature of social divisions. There is no doubt that the Pophams were in good standing as neighbours and held in genuine affection by the Cravens—Emily Mary expresses a deeply felt concern when, much later, Mrs Popham falls seriously ill. But the Pophams did not belong to the aristocracy, and could hardly have been a part of the Cravens' most intimate circle. In a letter to her sister Kate, Emily Mary, the kindest of women, refers to Mrs Popham rather patronisingly as, *my little friend Mrs. Popham.* She seems to have used the adjective not infrequently when referring to those to whom she was well disposed, but who were less than her social equals.

*Littlecote Park,
the home of Craven's neighbour,
Francis L Popham, Esq.*

Wild Darrell would quickly repay the faith shown in him by winning a three-horse race for two-year-olds at Newmarket, in 1854. He was then put into training under the day-to-day supervision of Popham's groom, Rickaby, and Craven's stablelads, who were Rickaby's sons. Popham still had no professional trainer,and Craven himself kept a close watch on the horse's progress during the severe winter of 1854–55,

---

[i] No further Craven exhibition entries have come to light.

Littlecote Park.

the famous Crimean War winter which put an end to the earlier spectacular victories and hampered the siege of Sebastopol that followed. Everywhere over England that winter frost and snow continued without a break throughout March and on into April. All the horses in training for the classic races had their excercise and gallops seriously curtailed by the weather. The Berkshire Downs suffered less than other places. While the Newmarket levels lay inches deep in snow, strong winds kept the high tops of the Downs fairly clear, and the mat of short thick grass.... too dry to freeze hard, made it possible to keep Wild Darrell in full work throughout the spring.[72]

The final weeks before the Derby saw a dramatic play of events. The bookies, knowing nothing about this dark horse's form, made him a rank outsider at odds of 66-1. Craven wagered a sporting £100 to win. But word of Wild Darrell's form began to spread, and Popham was approached by one Harry Hill, *a bookmaker and a singularly repulsive villain,*[73] and owner besides of another Derby hope, Kingstown, which he had backed heavily to win. Hill is said to have offered Popham £5,000 not to run Wild Darrell—an offer declined, of course, with contempt. Hill then sent in his gang of toughs to try and nobble Wild Darrell by sawing partway through the axle of his horsebox. As chance would have it, the day before Wild Darrell was due to leave for Epsom the horsebox was deployed to bring a sick bullock in from the pastures. The axle snapped; the horsebox turned over; the bullock was killed. To avoid risking the loss of a fortune, Hill was now obliged to hedge, backing Wild Darrell at whatever price was available. The odds shortened dramatically. *Wild Dayrell went to the post, for the Derby, in the finest condition possible, and his appearance was grand in the extreme.*[74] Racing under Popham's colours, Wild Darrell started as favourite at even money. He was ridden to a triumphant victory over Kingstown by the stablelad who had worked with him throughout the winter. The benign Craven, it was said, had not wanted to disappoint the boy by handing the horse over at the last minute to a professional jockey.

And of the name, Wild Darrell? Legend has it that one stormy winter's night, late in the reign of Queen Elizabeth I, a masked horseman appeared at the door of a midwife and bade her accompany him— blindfolded, for there was a need for secrecy, to attend *a lady of rank*, who had come to term. With some hesitation, and fearful, the midwife agreed. After a long journey the two arrived at a grand house, where the midwife found the pregnant woman waiting in her bedchamber, in the company of a man of *haughty and ferocious aspect*. The midwife delivered the woman of a child, a baby boy, which the man immediately tore from her and, *in spite of the intercession of the midwife, and the more piteous entreaties of the mother, thrust it into the grate, and raking the live coals upon it, soon put an end to its life.*

The unfortunate mother may have been the maid to this monster's wife. Horror-stricken, the midwife was once again blindfolded and returned to her home. The following day she made a deposition before a magistrate. From the time the journey had taken, and her description of some details she had noted about the grand house at the time her blindfold was removed, suspicion soon fell on 'Wild' Will Darrell, the owner of Littlecote Park. He was arrested and tried for murder, but escaped sentence allegedly by corrupting the judge. The judge's name was Sir John Popham, who shortly thereafter became the new owner of Littlecote Park! A few months later, Will Darrell broke his neck when he fell from his horse while out hunting. Littlecote thereafter remained the seat of the Popham family.

History or myth, two versions of this tale of Gothic horror occur in an appendix to an 1857 collection to the works of Sir Walter Scott. Darrell was the subject of a ballad by Scott included in his long narrative poem, *Rokeby,*[75] with which the Cravens were familiar. The name of Craven's neighbour's groom, who trained Wild Darrell was, we recall, *Rickaby*. Was the macabre pun of Craven's making? Or Popham's?

That summer, 1855, Kate Clarendon, Emily Mary's sister, went to stay with the Cravens at Ashdown. Her diary entry for 23rd August reads, *We heard today that Craven's and Mr Popham's horse Wild Dayrell the winner of the Derby had won a race at York which they cared very much about, as it was against a famous horse.*[76] The race was the Ebor St Leger, the horse he beat by two lengths was Oulston. Three days later Kate writes, *We went to Church in the morning &c &c had prayers and then walking about in the afternoon.... we went to see the famous Wild Dayrell in his Stables where he is returned quite safely after his successes.*

Having sired many a winner, Wild Darrell lived to be eighteen.

> *In the morning of the day on which he died, Thomas Hodgson, who had succeeded Rickaby as stud groom at Littlecote, entered Wild Dayrell's box, and found him perfectly well. He had emptied his manger to the last oat, and nothing indicated his approaching dissolution. When, however, Hodgson visited him again in the middle of the day, the great horse lay dead in his box. It was the opinion of the vet at Hungerford that apoplexy was the cause of his death.*[77]

Wild Darrell is the first Derby winner to have posed for the camera. Two versions of the photograph are found in the Craven portfolio. The first, as exhibited at the Photographic Society of Scotland, has Ashdown House as its backdrop. In the foreground the stud groom-cum-trainer, Rickaby, stands holding the horse's head. He is attended by his two sons. The second version reveals Craven's interest in the kind of experimentation that helped to expand the repertoire of photography in the 1850s. The house has been eliminated by applying an opaque medium to that area of the negative, so that the horse and its attendants stand starkly isolated against a featureless background. The photographs are obviously suggestive of English equestrian portraits of the eighteenth century. Craven lived surrounded by English sporting pictures, both in his own homes and in those of his friends and relatives. The complimentary versions of the portrait of Wild Darrell allude to these in general, and possibly to works by George Stubbs in particular. Stubbs, not alone of his contemporaries, invariably painted first the animals in his pictures, then added the lesser figures and the background. He also left a number of horse pictures 'unfinished', that is, without any background. These were not necessarily regarded as incomplete by his clients, who purchased and displayed them. In one case at least, *Mares and Foals without a Background* (c.1762) commissioned by the Marquess of Rockingham, the exclusion of the two mares at the centre of the picture leaves two groups of mares and foals at the flanks, which are the same groups, down to the details, as those found in *Mares and Foals in a River Landscape* (1760s) the only changes of note being those of the colour of the mare on the right of the pictures and the position of one of her hind legs. It is possibly no more than coincidence that Rockingham Castle and Craven's official seat at Combe Abbey were not many miles apart.

*Wild Dayrell,
winner of the Derby, 1855.*

Blocking out skies in order to render an overall even tone in place of incompletely registered clouds was a technique not uncommon even in the 1840s, and from the mid-1850s was further employed to allow for printing-in dramatic cloudscapes from a separate negative—as did Gustave Le Gray. But Craven had a further motive of his own for blocking out the landscape background. He did so in order to isolate and thus emphasize and empower his main subject, as may again be observed in one of his most striking works, *Study of a Gnarled Tree Trunk*, which survived in the folios in three prints of varying tonalities, the one of the deepest hue conveying the most powerful impact. As we shall see, the use of high contrast with suppressed intermediate tones (though usually without the application of opaquing medium to the negative, as in this case) also characterises a number of other masterworks by Craven.

81

83

Despite the sheer magnificence of many of the individual images that emerged from the Craven folios, there was little beyond the obvious—that he photographed mainly his family and his estate, and that he was interested in experimentation—to give them any sense of coherence as a group. The subsequent discovery of the great album, *A Record of the Earl of Craven's Photographic Experiments*, would change all that, and in addition, reveal through images alone the passage of a determining event in Craven's life. The album is split roughly into four sections: family and friends; the family home, Ashdown House, and the creation there of a grand parterre; the trees in the surrounding parkland; and the final leaves of the album which hold a few strays—including a print each of the *Vase of Ferns* and *A Brace and a Half of Partridges* (referred to above) *Wild Darrell* (background deleted) in Rickaby's charge, and a further portrait of Rickaby, topped by his stovepipe hat, and looking every bit the image of a man whose life has been fulfilled beyond expectation. He is flanked by his sons, Craven's stablelads, wearing their countryman's deerstalkers. The album as a whole, assembled at the end of Craven's life (it bears the date 1866, the year of his death) presents us with a certain number of difficulties. It is not exactly chronological; the sections are not quite defined; and it omits a number of key images present in the folios that are required to sequence Craven's work correctly. Furthermore, the family section seems to be put together according to whim—probably not by Craven himself. Lightly pencilled names—the album being unfinished—identify some of the subjects, but many of them are without name, making it difficult on occasion to separate the lookalike eldest daughters, in particular, and friends in general. None of the photographs bears a date, though circumstantial and external evidence helps to fix many of them within a fairly narrow timeframe.

Yet amidst all the uncertainties, one thing stands out very clearly: Craven's immediate, instinctive grasp of the particularity of photography as a medium. Whilst his photographs draw, with an intelligent and educated eye, on a wide range of art, Craven's *Photographic Experiments* are no imitation paintings, but are from the outset directed towards discovering and developing those characteristics in which photography distinguishes itself from the traditional medium—in the rendition of light and shade, in composition, and in the development of techniques which have no precise equivalent in painting, such as the use of differential planes of focus.

85

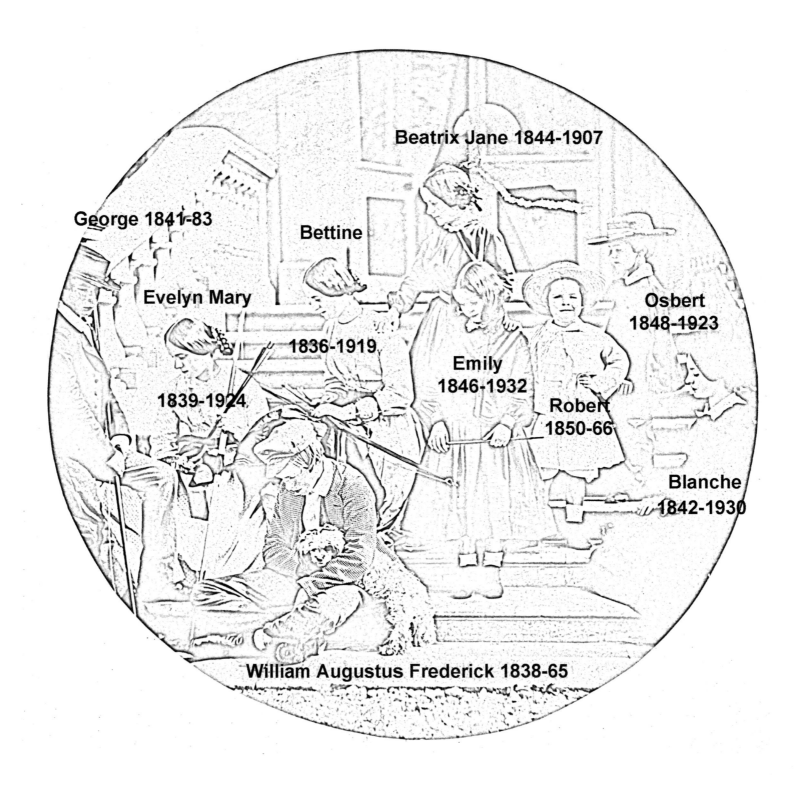

George 1841-83

Beatrix Jane 1844-1907

Bettine

Evelyn Mary

1836-1919

Osbert
1848-1923

Emily
1846-1932

1839-1924

Robert
1850-66

Blanche
1842-1930

William Augustus Frederick 1838-65

86

Bathed in the benign sun of an English summer's morning, the flight of stone steps descending from the back drawing-room of Ashdown House to the parterre below forms the backdrop to most of Craven's family portraits; the stage setting for his tableaux vivants. The mischievous-looking infant squinting into the glaring light, making himself the focal point of the image, the solo part with his siblings as chorus, is between three and four years old. He is Robert Walter, or Bobby, the Cravens' last and youngest of nine. Born in January 1850, Bobby is about three-and-a-half at the time of the photograph, taken in the summer of 1853. His life would be tragically brief, snuffed out far from home at the age of sixteen, shortly before his father's death.

Of the three toxophilites (the bow symbolising the ancient order, and the right of every Englishman owning a hundred acres of land to use it to hunt the beasts of the field) the lad on the left wearing the straw boater is George Grimston (b.1841) and the two girls are Elizabeth Charlotte Louisa, or Bettine (b.1836) with Evelyn Mary (b.1839) diagonally above her.[i] Below them, gripping the dog (a Bichon?) in a ferocious stranglehold to restrain its movement for the duration of the exposure, is William Augustus Frederick, Viscount Uffington, known as Uffie (b.1838). Uffie, the eldest son and heir, would not live to inherit. The Cravens were relatively fortunate in terms of child mortality statistics of the mid-nineteenth century. Only the first and last of nine would die before gaining their majority. There are no tales of pregnancies that failed to come to term, or of children that died in infancy. Aside from George, who died aged forty-two, the remaining six of this generation would live well into the twentieth century, three of them long enough to witness the end of Ashdown as the family home. At the summit of the pictorial pyramid is Beatrix Jane, or Beattie (b.1844) with Emily Georgiana (b.1846) below her. To the left of the infant Bobby are Osbert William, or Obbie (b.1848) and Blanche (b.1842).

---

[i] Computer enhancement confirms that the girl identified here as Evelyn Mary, also seen in a solo portrait in which she is identified by name, has much shorter tresses than her sister.

The close fit of the figures within the frame seems to indicate that the tondo, or roundel, was planned; yet it is just possible that it was fortuitous: the result of damage to the edges of a unique print.[i] The figuration as a formal group portrait could have been borrowed from painting, or equally, it could have been inspired by some of the group portraits—in particular, that of the Adamson Family—executed by the great Scottish calotypist, David Octavius Hill, which Craven might well have seen. Like the Adamsons, the Craven children have been carefully posed in advance—except for Bobby, much too excited—with their eyes cast downwards, enabling them to hold their positions comfortably in the glaring sunlight during the exposure. One can sense Craven, the stern but adoring and adored father, then turning his attention to the infant, coaxing him into posing. Bobby is photographed in the kind of spontaneous gesture rarely captured in the era before the introduction of instantaneous shutters.

The ritual begins: the dark-slide is loaded; the sheath is drawn; the children are called to attention; the lens is uncapped, the plate exposed; the sheath is safely reinserted into the dark-slide. The photo-call is over. It was the kind of charade that was so much enjoyed by Victorian families. In the case of Craven, such participation encouraged two of his children, Evelyn Mary and Obbie, to take up photography themselves, though they were not, alas, touched with their father's genius.

But whatever outside influences may have born in on this exceptional image, the most fundamental element is Craven's invention alone, and it chimes perfectly with the central notion of his photographic opus as autobiography. The image is of a unique architectural structure. Literally so. The composition of the group portrait appears to be a cryptic reference to Ashdown House itself, built by the 1st Earl of Craven in the seventeenth century, which was loved and favoured as the family home over the vast and unmanageable Combe Abbey. The invention is a pure artist's conceit: by transposing the group portrait laterally, the placing of the children can be seen to match closely the lines of the chimney pieces as they appear in an image of the house that Craven would not make until two years later—but which he had already registered, if only subconsciously

---

[i] There are quite extensive surface markings on the print and a section of the emulsion is missing in the top right quarter.

The tondo is not the only reference to the history and nobility of his family to be discovered in Craven's work, nor is it the only one to contain such occlusion. One leaf of the album is mounted with a group of three photographic copies, of which the centrepiece is from an engraving of Craven's ancestor, the 1st Earl, armoured and mounted. To the right is the family's heraldic shield under an earl's coronet, encircled by the so-called slughorn or motto, *Virtus in Actione Consistit* - Virtue Consists in Action. To the left is the cypher of William Craven the photographer, under an earl's coronet, with its heraldic signature of five small orbs. The cypher itself, as we have seen, is an elaborately figured encryption of the Craven name.

As the tondo points to the cypher, so the cypher anticipates the design of the parterre at Ashdown, that will commence construction the following year, and become the subject of some of Craven's most enduring imagery.

Children as individuals occupy only a minor niche in the history of portraiture before the coming of photography. As a genre child portraiture was the creation of the daguerreotype, and the thousands of images of children that survive from the 1840s and 1850s are amongst its most precious legacies. Despite the appearance of solemnity and quiescence engendered by the duration of the exposure in front of the camera, the children's air of innocence remains intact, whereas the majority of adult sitters seem either to be acting up for the camera—Baudelaire caustically described them as grimacing—or appear sulkily compliant while trying to maintain their dignity. Up to the mid-1850s photography on paper was almost entirely preoccupied with topography and architecture; portraiture was very much in the minority; and of the calotypists of the previous decade only Hill and Adamson and Talbot's kinsman, John Dillwyn Llewelyn, together with his sister Mary, come to mind as significant photographers of children, alongside the far more numerous adult subjects. However, Craven's photographs of his own children from 1853 to around 1857 appear to be unique. The cumbersome nature of the process placed constraints on the photographer, yet amongst Craven's images of his own children and of his nieces are a group in which they appear completely unselfconscious in the presence of the camera, and are lost in their own thoughts and preoccupations. The difficulties confronting Craven were no less than those of other photographers using the same kind of equipment. But Craven drew on one special advantage: he had an exceptionally close bond with his children, in defiance of the conventions. The children of the upper classes would normally be brought up in the care of servants, their world bounded by nursery and nanny—a surrogate mother—and governess, with restricted access to their parents until, at a still tender age, the boys would be sent to boarding school, while the girls began their grooming for entry into society and the marriage market. Craven's images of his children speak of his intimacy with them, his concern for their development as individuals, as well as speaking eloquently of his own character, where there is no other testimony. The images are evidence of the warmth and tenderness of his love for them, of his gentleness towards them, and of his proximity to them. Without the mutual affection of which these sweet images are the expression, they would never have succeeded in their being. It is worth remarking that many of the most enduring images of the mid-nineteenth century were created by those who were, like Craven, close to their subjects, adult or child. In the wake of Craven came Lewis Carroll with his own family, as well as the Hatches, Liddells and Kitchins; Lady Clementina Hawarden with her daughters; Julia Margaret Cameron with her grand circle of neighbours and friends, and their children.

Craven ventured beyond the immediate neighbourhood of Ashdown with his camera on only one identifiable occasion, almost certainly in the summer of 1854, and that was on a fishing trip. Whilst the location of the two resulting (or only surviving?) photographs is unknown, it was certainly not close by, for there were no rivers close to Ashdown that would have been suited that particular day's outing. Fly fishing was then the new sport of gentlemen, and the pair of gillies posed outside the thatched fishing lodge are holding heavy two-handed salmon rods between fifteen and eighteen feet in length, made of shaved greenheart. They are far too long for use on the nearby tributaries of the Thames. As for the Thames itself, by the 1850s it was no longer a salmon river. Industrial pollution had all but killed off life in the river; and besides, navigation locks and weirs prevented returning salmon from moving upstream to their spawning redds.

The design of the windows of the lodge shows the group portrait to be one of a pair with that of the gillies standing in front of the lodge The group of fishermen is surely a masterpiece of its kind, the archetypal image of the all-male club. These are men who are relaxed, self-assured, at ease with themselves and their aristocratic world, stylish even in their fishing gear—the character in the foreground especially so, with his thigh-length leather waders, woven cane creel, and gold watch chain (known as an 'Albert' after the Prince Consort, who made a fashion accessory of watch and fob chains) looped across the waistcoat of his elegantly checked tweed suiting. Having set up his subjects in a cruciform composition, Craven, for some inexplicable reason austerely dark-suited on this warm summer's day, enters the picture from the right a fractional moment before his assistant uncaps the lens. At the moment of exposure it seems that Craven has not yet quite steadied his stance, and his outline is slightly blurred with movement, in contrast to the sharp outlines of his companions.

The composition of the picture is both ambitious and complex, and so unusual in its structure that it is difficult to believe that Craven had not taken instruction from the work of Rembrandt. If this seems a speculation too far, it should be said that in her travel diaries of 1837, Emily Mary comments on Rubens and Van Dyke in Antwerp, then on Rembrandt's *dissection of a man* (as she describes it) at Rotterdam (being either *The Anatomy Lesson of Dr. Tulp* or that of *Dr. van der Meer*). And if the idea be not considered too profane: the massing of the figures of Craven's friends seems to owe much to that in Rembrandt's *The Raising of the Cross*, as well as *The Prodigal Son with the Loose Women*, and other compositions particular to Rembrandt. Craven's construction is then set against the strong, convergent lines behind the men, with himself balancing the out-of-focus darkness of the servant group at left.

Faintly pencilled names on the margin of the album leaf below the print identify the members of the fishing party. The sprawling figure is Lord Tamworth. Above him to the right, sporting a similar tweed, is a somewhat dour-looking Frederick Keppel Craven (1811–64) the youngest brother of the photographer. The figure to the rear, holding his weighty greenheart aloft in a remarkably steady grip, is pencilled in as Sir F. Bathurst. This is yet another Frederick, and the sureness of his grip is no surprise, for he is Sir Frederick Hutchison Hervey-Bathurst (1807–81) one of Craven's Old Etonian companions and a first class batsman, who played for the Marylebone Cricket Club and Hampshire. Finally, there is the figure on the left of the picture, who is identified only as W. Boothby. The image is one full of unconscious foreboding, for—as we shall see—the lives of three of the five would soon be shadowed by tragedy, beginning with Boothby, on the point of leaving to join his regiment in the Crimea. On 28th March 1854, France and Britain declared war on Russia. It was the start of the cruel conflict that forms a dark backdrop to all the events of the mid-1850s. For those who, like the Cravens, were not involved at first hand, early reports of the campaign were of limited significance, though they were closer to events than most: Emily Mary Craven's sister, Katharine—Kate—was the wife of George Villiers, 4th Earl of Clarendon, who was Secretary of State for foreign affairs (or in today's usage, Foreign Secretary) at the outbreak of the Crimean War. In most respects, however, life continued without undue disturbance—apart, that is, from the voice of a populace clamouring for a war it would soon come to regret. For the Cravens, their eldest daughter was about to become a debutante. Two days after the declaration of war, with Elizabeth Craven, known in the family as Bettine, approaching her eighteenth birthday, Kate Clarendon noted in her diary:

> *Thurs. 30th March 1854. The Queen's first Drawing Room this year - Elizabeth Craven was presented.*

> *Sat. 1st April. We had dinner at home and a tail afterwards at which Elizabeth Craven made her first appearance in London.*

And Bettine's coming-out ball was certainly an occasion to be marked:

> *Wedn. 24th May 1854. I don't often think it worthwhile to mention Balls and Parties unless something particular happens at them, but today there was a Ball of Balls and most interesting to one. Emily Craven's first ball for Elizabeth Craven it was <u>exceptionally</u> brilliant, and splendidly done and their home did look lovely!! -* [78]

107

In the Crimea, there was only limited skirmishing throughout that summer as the Allied forces continued their build-up, and the fearful toll that dysentery and cholera exacted on the ordinary troops did little to dampen the British public's ill-judged enthusiasm for the war. Neither were the general public or the ruling classes yet fully cognisant of the gross mismanagement of the supply lines by the military authorities, nor of the incompetence of Britain's aging generals, some of whom had last seen action at the Battle of Waterloo, forty years earlier. Consequently, a still untroubled Kate Clarendon was able to inform her diary on 25th October, 1854, that:

Today as we heard afterwards was the day of the battle of Balaclava and Lord
Cardigan's gallant charge with the Light Cavalry.

The carnage suffered by the Light Brigade at Balaclava is too infamous a story to require repeating here. In the Battle of Inkerman that followed on 5th November the Allies were victorious, but the tally of death and mutilation was appalling. At home (in Russia, as much as Britain, France and Turkey) the costs of war began to be counted in personal terms. Boothby was badly hurt, but fortunate enough—it seemed at first sight—to be repatriated, rather than suffer the scourge of the notorious hospital at Scutari. However, on 12th January, 1855, a newly aware Kate Clarendon recorded in her diary:

A day or two ago I got a letter from Emily Craven so angry with the treatment
which the wounded and sick officers have received at the Horse Guards!
- and she is right to be angry, for it seems to be disgraceful - ordered
up by a particular day to be examined - then told that the medical board
was not there to examine them, appointed for two days later at
whatever inconvenience, expense or even peril to the invalids - when
they appeared there kept waiting, and worse than all so brutally examined,
that poor Mr. Boothby who had lost his foot at Inkerman was forced to
undo the bandages at torture and injury to the limb - for what? - to see that
the foot was off I suppose!! [79]

Roger Fenton, c.1855, attributed
to Dr Hugh Welch Diamond.

A month after this frightful scene took place the photographer, Roger Fenton, with the active encouragement of Prince Albert, took ship for the Crimea.

108

Roger Fenton was the main driving force behind the establishment of the Photographic Society of London in 1853, and the man who in the 1850s would bestride the world of British photography as the most accomplished of his generation; a romantic; a man dedicated to the elevation of photography to the status of art in the minds of the public. A group of images by Fenton was among the most important photographs discovered in Craven's collection of the works of his contemporaries.

Born to a wealthy Northern family of bankers, landowners and industrialists, Roger Fenton studied painting in Paris in the mid-1840s, and subsequently in London under the history painter Charles Lucy. His first known photographs date from 1852. During the following decade Fenton mastered every branch of photography to which he addressed himself. His landscapes and studies of romantic ruins may have subscribed nominally to conventional ideals of the picturesque, but they were attained with such exquisite choice of moment when it came to the effects created by the ambient light that one is left wondering how much time he spent contemplating each of his subjects before exposing a negative. By contrast, his other architectural photographs, notably those of grand country houses, showed a powerful originality that owed nothing to painterly composition, but belonged to an emerging photographic aesthetic. His appointment as official photographer to the British Museum generated a series of studies of sculpture of monolithic intensity. He created a group of mysterious and brooding orientalist tableaux; and his still-lifes contain fruit so rounded and luscious that one might almost pick the grapes off the surface of the print. His photography brought him into close contact with the royal family, and his portraits of Queen Victoria and her family are of an easy and intimate nature. But his fame amongst a wider public in the 1850s rested on photography of quite a different kind. On September 1, 1855, the *Art-Journal* reported:

Roger Fenton:
Pool below the Strid

> *Mr. Roger Fenton, the distinguished photographist, has recently returned from the*
> *Crimea, with a large number of admirable photographs of incidents and events connected*
> *with the siege of Sebastopol, Mr. Fenton has had, we believe, unusual facilities for*
> *accomplishing his labours, and the result is a series of subjects as novel as they will be found*
> *interesting, if we may judge from those submitted to us. Messrs Agnew & Sons have,*
> *we understand, purchased the copyright in these scenes, with a view to publication;*
> *prior to which, however, they will be publicly exhibited.*

Roger Fenton: Rievaulx Abbey.

The difficulties that had been involved in this enterprise can hardly be overstated. Quite apart from the obvious dangers of working at the war front, and of exposure to infection and disease—Fenton contracted cholera and was fortunate to survive—there was the problem of contending with the extraordinarily cumbersome wet-collodion process. In order to be able to move from one location to another carrying his five cameras of different sizes, crate-loads of glass plates, plus a veritable laboratory for the preparation, development and printing of his negatives, Fenton required some form of vehicle and shelter more substantial than that offered by the photographer's travelling dark-tent of the kind then generally available. His needs were fulfilled by converting a wine merchant's delivery van into what Fenton called his 'photographic van'. He later described his makeshift quarters to the members of the Photographic Society:

Roger Fenton's photographic van with his assistant, Marcus Sparling, in the driving seat. This wood engraving, taken from a photograph, appeared in the Illustrated London News.

> *When it entered into the service of art, a fresh top was made for it, so as to convert it into a dark room, panes of yellow glass, with shutters, were fixed in the sides; a bed was constructed for it, which folded up into a very small space under the bench at the upper end; round the top were cisterns for distilled and for ordinary water, and a shelf for books. On the sides were places for fixing the gutta-percha baths, glass-dippers, knives forks and spoons. The kettle and cups hung from the roof. On the floor, under the trough for receiving waste water, was a frame with holes, in which were fitted the heavier bottles. This frame had at night to be lifted up and placed on the working bench with the cameras, to make room for the bed, the furniture of which was, during the day, contained in the box under the driving seat.[80]*

From time to time the van, evidently mistaken for an ammunition wagon if not for some new infernal engine of war, came under enemy fire. It once lost its roof.

Whether Fenton was already contemplating an expedition to the Crimea when he had the van tricked out is not known, but it passed its road trials with flying colours some four months earlier on a less hazardous journey, trundling its way across the North of England. Although not all the images that Craven acquired from Fenton can be dated with certainty, Valerie Lloyd dates the numinous image of the Gothic ruins of Rievaulx Abbey to this trip, undertaken in September, 1854.[81] Bolton Abbey was also on the itinerary; and so the *Pool below the Strid*—of which Craven owned a print—belongs to the same group of images, the Strid being a narrow, seething chasm into which the waters of the River Wharfe are channelled, a short walk from Bolton Abbey. Craven also owned several of Fenton's views of the Wharfe, which descends upon Bolton Abbey from the Yorkshire Dales to the north-west.

111

We can safely conclude, therefore, that Craven and Fenton—already well acquainted—were in close contact at this period.

Was the idea of the van the outcome of conversations between the two photographers, or did Craven take inspiration from Fenton? It is unlikely to have been the other way about, for Fenton was the more experienced, his programme was the more ambitious and his practical requirements for mobility were far more pressing. But whichever it was, Craven commissioned a fancy, custom-built version of the photographic van for his own use at about the same time as Fenton undertook the conversion of his second-hand wine merchant's vehicle.

There is nothing to suggest that Craven's elegant van ever travelled beyond the confines of the Ashdown estate, or was ever endangered by anything more lethal than a dose of birdshot. It was a unique indulgence, and is now a piece of photographic lore: no other such van is known to have been built at the time. One of Craven's grandsons left a vivid account of the van, which incorporated an innovation that even Fenton had not considered—the van as mobile camera.

The hand camera did not then exist. Grandpapa's Kodak was a caravan - four-wheeled and horse drawn - camera and darkroom combined. The lens projected from the front of the vehicle, which at the back was fitted with double doors so that the operator could go in or come out without danger of daylight interference. He drove in state to whatever object he wanted to photograph, took out the horse because it obstructed the lens's view, and then shut himself into the caravan to prepare and sensitise the plate by the elaborate wet Collodion process then in vogue; the ready-made dry plate being as yet unknown. Having set up the prepared plate upon a stand or easel at the correct focal distance, he came out into the open to uncap the lens for the prolonged exposure then necessary. This done, he went inside again to develop, fix and wash the plate, and then, and not till then he drove home to make at his leisure whatever prints from the negative he required. In those days snapshotting demanded both determination and diligence, much time, no little outlay, and quite a lot of luck.[82]

Like Fenton, and all ambitious photographers at that time, Craven had cameras of several different formats. Enlarging photographs beyond the size of the original camera negative would have resulted in the aggrandisement of such existing defects as fall-off in lens edge-definition—already a problem to be contended with, as well as making the kind of comets described earlier more prominent. The obvious alternative, of making enlarged copy negatives from an existing print by rephotographing on to a larger format was equally undesirable, since however perfect the print the quality of the copy would always have been inferior to the original. Thus, amongst the early criteria for selecting a camera of any given negative format would have been the desired size of the final print. Were it not that a one-to-one print—a contact print—produced an infinitely superior result to an enlargement, it would be difficult to account for the sanity of a man like Francis Frith, bearing his burden of a 16x20 camera down the Valley of the Nile in a hundred degrees of heat. Craven, though he may perhaps have lacked artistic confidence in the early days of his work, clearly harboured no doubts about his ability to handle the outsized equipment he soon commissioned, which was equal to the largest format then in use. His manual dexterity has been described earlier. Even so, the difficulties of achieving an even coating of emulsion on a 18x24-inch (45x60 cm.) glass plate weighing perhaps two kilos, and of manhandling it on to the easel of the van-camera without risk of damage would have been formidable and must have constrained its use. Moreover, the van-camera would have made for an unusually elevated point of view. This did, as we shall see, turn out to be of advantage in particular cases, but on other occasions it would have made for unacceptable limitations that could be overcome only by the alternative use of more conventional apparatus.

Craven's van survives only as the subject of the striking and austere photograph that its owner made of it early in the winter of 1854–55, before the coming of the snows that would soon help Wild Darrell to victory in the Derby. The skill of the coachbuilding and the high finish are in marked contrast to Fenton's workaday vehicle. Sitting on the ground with their backs to the great rear wheel are Craven's two eldest sons: on the right, Uffie, with his signature flat cap and Eton collar; on the left, George, clutching a small dog in his lap. At the extreme left of frame the downed tree trunks are evidence of the work going on in Ashdown Park at the time (of which, more to come). Nothing is known of the fate of the magnificent vehicle after the death of Craven but, built to last, yet with its original purpose gone, it probably declined into ignominious old age as a farm vehicle on the Ashdown estate.

It was a cruel stroke of fate that denied Craven the opportunity of photographing the van before the onset of winter. While his friend Roger Fenton was composing pictures of Gothic ruins in the North, Craven, then two months past his forty-fifth birthday and with everything to live for—wealth, position, a loving wife and children, his accomplishments as a sportsman, and a way of life that must have been the envy of many—was felled by a stroke. Kate Clarendon's diary reported:

Sat 9th Sept 1854

Alarming attack of Craven's was announced to Mama - it must have taken place last
Thursday at Ashdowne - one side affected, speech and face a little, but mind and sight not
at all, it is a paralytic seizure but from the accounts we hope a ~~slight one~~ not a very severe one [i]

The subsequent news is tentatively optimistic:

Thurs 14th September

We received excellent accts of Craven

Six weeks after the stroke the crisis is evidently past. Emily Mary feels confident enough to leave
Craven and spend a night in London. For such a brief visit she stays with Kate, rather than opening up
her own house nearby.

Monday 23rd Oct 1854

Emily Craven [ii] *and Elizabeth came for one night - Emily brought a very good*
account of Craven [83]

For the time being the worst was over—for Craven, at least. Two days later came the disastrous charge
of the Light Brigade. Ten days after that his friend Boothby had his foot blown off at the Battle of
Inkerman. By early winter Craven had resumed his photography, though was probably neither hunting
nor shooting. Quite apart from his convalescence, the coldest winter in a decade was setting in early,
putting a blight on field sports. As early in the season as 28th November Kate Clarendon's diary notes:

The hunting a little dubious - but it was at last decided that the frost was not sufficiently
gone to make it safe. [84]

The winter of 1854 would be a long and bitter one.

---

[i] Kate always misspells Ashdown, and *a slight one* is scored through thus.
[ii] Kate refers to her sister as Emily Craven to differentiate her from her sister-in-law, also Emily.

Combe Abbey, c.1860. Photo by Wingrave of Coventry.

Of the Craven family's three main residences,[i] Hamstead Marshall continued to be occupied by the photographer's mother, Louisa, after the death of his father. Ashdown, manageable, convenient both to London and to the court at Windsor Castle, was considered by Emily Mary to be the home best suited to the raising of her children. The third residence, Combe Abbey, the official seat of the Craven family, was a problem. By origin a Cistercian monastery dating from shortly after the Norman Conquest, the abbey was seized by Henry VIII in 1539, during the general dissolution of the monasteries, and subsequently purchased by the Craven family early in the seventeenth century. When the 2nd Earl inherited Combe Abbey in 1825, it was an assemblage of, *the late Gothic of the cloisters, the Jacobean features of the courtyard and the south-west building, and by the full Palladianism of the west and north elevation.*[85] As a group of buildings it may have been imposing, but successive additions had made it increasingly unliveable. There could be no question of disposing of Combe, which represented a continuum through successive generations of Cravens, yet Emily Mary disliked the place and saw it only as a drain on family resources. Whilst Craven might long since have relieved himself of his burden of inherited debt, he had no means of raising anew the kind of capital sum needed to modernise Combe, and one can only suppose that it was pride that prevented him writing the letter that the forthright Emily Mary must herself have addressed with some reluctance to the fashionable architect, Edward Blore, who had only recently added a third storey to The Grove, the home of her sister and brother-law, the Clarendons.

Combe Abbey, Monday Febry 14th 1842

Dear Sir

Ever since the Earl and I have seen the wonders that you have produced at the Grove, we have been most anxious to have the benefit of your opinion about this old house which we are extremely anxious to make more convenient and if possible less expensive for at present it is so straggling a building that without having much available room we find the keeping it in proper repair as more than we can.... afford. Would you have the kindness

---

[i] Charles Street, the London residence, was more of a socially necessity than a real home.

Combe Abbey, an interior, c.1860. Stereophoto by Wingrave of Coventry.

to attempt helping us and do you think you be able to pay us a visit any time
before the end of the month....

Yours very truly

Emily M Craven[86]

It is a revealing document. People like the Cravens were not generally given to public discussion about what they could or could not afford. The reason for approaching Edward Blore, aside from his successful addition to The Grove, was probably that he had acquired a reputation for being careful with his clients' money. It was Blore who was appointed to complete the last phase of the conversion of Buckingham House, purchased by George III for Queen Charlotte as her town-house, into Buckingham Palace, after Nash was fired for vastly exceeding his estimates. We can assume that Blore did not accept the commission from the Cravens because he was too busy, which may have turned out to be just as well. His work on Buckingham Palace was not universally admired for its design so much as for its economies; his 1841 rebuild of the Church of St Mary's, Chepstow was criticised for having largely erased the character of the original Norman structure; his plans for Government House, Sydney, Australia, constructed between 1837 and 1843, though in the fashionable style of the Gothic Revival, were somewhat tired. In 1843, Blore also worked on St John the Evangelist's at Cinderford, and there were numerous other projects keeping him busy at that period. In the event, twenty years would elapse before the refurbishment and extension of Combe Abbey was placed in the hands of William Eden Nesfield— associate of Barry, designer of the Houses of Parliament—and a leading enthusiast of the Gothic Revival.[i]

William Eden Nesfield was one of two sons of William Andrews Nesfield, who was in turn a soldier, painter, and finally a garden architect. Obscure in the first occupation, well-regarded in the second—he was a friend of JMW Turner, and a painter of vigorous watercolours of seascapes and waterfalls that were much commended by John Ruskin—Nesfield senior would achieved a considerable reputation as one of the finest garden architects of the mid-century. Amongst his public commissions, he was responsible in part for the design of Regent's Park, and he drew up the original designs for Kew. Privately, he was much employed by the aristocracy, hence his name would have been familiar to Craven. Nesfield redesigned gardens at Arundel Castle and Castle Howard, amongst other noble houses, before being employed at Combe Abbey, the latter in partnership with his son, who also worked on the building itself, adding a new wing to it.

---

[i] Later in Nesfield's career, his enthusiasm for the Gothic spent, he became a partner of Norman Shaw.

The avenue of limes.

English garden design in the nineteenth century became increasingly eclectic, embracing the garden as formal design, in the manner of the seventeenth century and before; the garden as natural landscape, as developed by William Kent and Capability Brown in the eighteenth century; the newly developed flower garden, which reflected the increased availability of many exotic varieties previously unseen in the British Isles; and the garden as setting for neo-classical temples, and for imported ideas, such as chinoiserie. Under the influence of Humphry Repton, many English gardens began to encompass several of these elements. Notably, Repton re-introduced the use of the terrace, or the parterre, as an extension of the house, creating an enrichment of the foreground (as seen from the house) with a more natural landscape beyond. William Andrews Nesfield was noted particularly for his use of terraces and parterres, and indeed he would in due course embellish Combe Abbey with a new terrace. Long before the reconstruction of Combe Abbey however, the Cravens, faced with economic reality, gave priority to home over official seat. William Andrews Nesfield—and presumably his then twenty-year-old son, William Eden Nesfield—began work on a grand redesign of the gardens at Ashdown in the summer of 1854. Though no written documentation has come to light relating to the remaking of the gardens, Craven's photographs—true to the thesis that they constitute a form of memoir—provide us with a detailed account of the progress of the work.

The first image in the chronology is taken from the roof terrace surrounding the lantern at the top of the house, providing a view along the length of the avenue of lime trees at the rear of the house and beyond, to the distant line of the Berkshire Downs. The photograph is taken in high summer—the trees are in full leaf. The lawns in the foreground are as yet undisturbed, though at least some part of the new border of yew that will form a hedge defining the shape of the planned parterre has already been planted. The plans call for the felling of a considerable number of trees to tidy up the backdrop to the formal garden, and the opportunity is seized to thin out surrounding woodlands where necessary to maintain their health. Craven's stroke intervenes after the view from the roof terrace, and it is early winter before he is well enough to continue with his photography. The stripped trunks of some of the felled trees are visible in the left background of the later image of the photographic van, and others appear in many more of the treescapes taken in the course of the winter of 1854–55 and through the summer of 1855.

121

Craven's trees are the first of the two main subjects (the second being the parterre) that will preoccupy him through almost a year commencing November or December 1854. Out of a setting of no more than a few acres close to the house he succeeds in creating such a rich variety of imagery as would alone justify the word *Experiments* in the title of his album. Some of the total of forty images of trees, including variations on a theme, are contained in the album itself. The remainder were discovered in the folios, mainly on card mounts, some of which are watermarked *Whatman 1855*. A number of these mounts are embossed with Craven's seal. Craven made a point of employing the most excellent tools available for the job in hand—ancient armour for tournaments, Holtzapffel lathes for turning, and now cameras and lenses. The photographs of trees are captured on cameras of three separate formats, [i] two at least being custom-built. While the largest horizontals were taken with the van-camera, utilising its maximum capability of 24-inches (60cm.) square, the indications are that some of the most striking images of those in the vertical 16x12 inch (40x30cm.) format were taken from the van, too. A further group are derived from a camera built specifically for landscapes employing a horizontal format of some 11x14-inches (27.5x35cm.) or a 14x14-inch camera, though the prints of many of the images from this camera, of whichever format, have been radically trimmed down to new compositions.

The balance of Craven's 16x12 tree images were taken on another of his idiosyncratic pieces of equipment, covering the same formats as the van, but engineered to conquer finally the difficulties of achieving the ideal point of view with cameras that were cumbersome and difficult to manoeuvre. It is not the kind of criterion that today, with the casual use of highly portable miniature cameras, film or digital, would readily strike one as being of major significance when deciding on how to compose a picture. Similarly, we have long since come to expect lenses that are manufactured to the highest degree of optical perfection, distortion free, rendering a perfectly flat field which is sharp all the way to the edges of the picture, in which the spectral colours all converge at the same plane of focus, and are rendered with a degree of contrast adequate to give a sense of solidity to the resulting image. In Craven's day such virtuous lenses did not exist, and compromises which affected the aesthetic outcome often had to be made in the design of lenses, which resulted in making them more suited to a single predetermined purpose than to general use in a wide variety of circumstances.

The camera-mobile, as one might call it, was vast and imposing, a beautifully constructed brass-bound sliding-box camera, with rack-and-pinion back-focusing along brass guide rails. The basic design was fairly conventional in the days before the general use of bellows cameras, but the size of the camera and the novel carriagework were not.

---

[i] There was possibly a fourth, smaller format camera that Craven used for the 'snaps' of the children and later on other family and friends.

The camera is seen mounted on wheels of some five-foot (150cm.) diameter (from which it could conveniently be dismounted) which appear to have been made for a curricle, a fast-moving gentleman's two-wheeled carriage. It is seated on a platform mounted on elliptical springs, as the chassis of the curricle would have been. At the rear, there is a short shaft with handles, allowing the carriage to be pulled by two assistants—we may be sure that Craven himself, after his stroke, did not help in the heavy work. With the camera-mobile aligned for an exposure, it was stabilised on four legs on ball-and-socket joints, found at the corners of the platform. As he stands behind the camera, Craven's head proportionate to the back of the camera indicates a format of the same gigantic dimensions as the van-camera, that is, 24-inches (60 cm.) square. The square aperture of the camera back would have allowed for the insertion of plate-holders for horizontal or vertical framing of an image, these options being marked out on the ground-glass focusing screen to ensure accuracy of framing. The camera featured a lens panel (termed a 'rising and cross front') mounted in grooves, allowing the lens a limited range of vertical and horizontal displacement.[i] This was still a fairly novel feature on cameras of the era, though significantly, it was included in Scott Archer's design for a portable landscape camera.[87] A similar capability for adjusting the position of the lens relative to the plate was a feature of the van-camera, though there achieved by adjustment of the plate itself—Bombardier describes an 'easel', implying an arrangement based on a painter's easel. Like the van and the camera, the brass-bound landscape lens—a double achromat, selected for its sharpness of image— would need to have been specially made. Lenses of this dimension—in its housing it is noticeably larger than Craven's head—were not available off the shelf, but would have been computed and ground to order. Its focal length would have been in excess of 30-inches (75cm.) probably with a maximum nominal aperture of f/5.6 or f/8—nominal, because for landscape work it would always have been employed at a far smaller aperture to eliminate any loss of sharpness in the image, especially at the outer rim of the lens. The smaller aperture would also increase depth of field, and improve image contrast and flatness of field. The consequent increase in exposure time would have been of no consequence, the subject being immobile. Lenses at this period were commonly described not by focal length or f/stop but by the diameter of the front glass.[ii]

---

[i] The presence of this design feature in Craven's camera and its significance explained below.

[ii] These became and remain the standard terms for describing lenses. Focal length is the distance from the film plane, with the camera focused on infinity, to the nodal point, or central point of focus of the lens. f/stop is focal length divided by diameter of lens.

The gigantic lens, interchangeable between van and camera-mobile, will have had a diameter of six to eight inches (15 to 20cm.) at full aperture.[i] Craven would also have had shorter focal length lenses suited to the lesser negative formats, using the same cameras. It was not unusual to insert one or more reducing kits, or slip frames, into the plate holder to enable the use of a camera to make negative of less than the maximum size it was designed for, and many of Craven's masterworks were taken on 16x12-inch (40x30cm.) negatives, an exceptionally large number of them in vertical format.

Some of concerns that had to be addressed by photographers seeking technical mastery of their medium in the wet-collodion era were best described—and articulated in an entertaining manner easily accessible to the laity—in the writings of one of the great topographical photographers of the 1850s, Francis Frith. In 1856, Frith, a successful entrepreneur turned photographer, embarked on the first of what would be three trips to the Middle East, convinced that there was a niche market for high quality photographs produced on an industrial scale. He was right; there was and he filled it, and he was praised, besides, for the splendour of his work. Frith modelled his three expeditions to the Middle East, and his marketing methods, on the similar enterprise undertaken by the Scottish artist, David Roberts, in 1838, in the course of which Roberts produced what proved to be a highly popular set of folio-size coloured lithographs. The publication of these was meticulously planned, with almost 250 prints being issued in forty partworks over a period of eight years, 1842–49, supported by a learned text leaning heavily on biblical reference. The partwork was followed by a bound six-volume set. It was without doubt one of the greatest and most ambitious feats of publishing of the nineteenth century.

14x14 inch (35x35 cm.) plate holder with reducing kit.

Like Craven, Frith photographed on several different negative formats. The largest was 16x20 inches (40x50cm.) in which he produced a folio of majestic images of the Valley of Kings. In 1858–60, following their success as partworks, Frith's smaller 8x10-inch (20x25cm.) photographs, with accompanying text, were published as a two-volume set entitled *Egypt and Palestine Photographed and Described*. Further publications followed. In addition, Frith took stereoscopic views, which were published as stereo-cards, slides and even book illustrations. In the introduction and text to *Egypt and Palestine* Frith, a natural storyteller, wrote with humour and sometimes with exasperation of his labours:

---

[i] In his *Manual of Photographic Manipulation*, 1858, (p.176) Lake Price gives six and eight inches as the diameters of the lenses used for extra large images of the Louvre. These could only be those taken by Edouard Baldus in 1854, and they were of the same approximate dimensions as Craven's largest images. The French camera-maker, Plagniol, exhibited a 24-inch square camera with a double-achromat lens of eight-inch diameter at the Great Exhibition of 1851.

A photographer only knows - he only can appreciate the difficulty of getting a view
into the camera; foregrounds are especially perverse; distance too near or too far;
the falling away of the ground; the intervention of some brick wall or other
commonplace object, which an artist would simply omit; - some or all of these
things (with plenty others of a similar character) are the rules not the exception.
I have often thought, when manoevring about for a position for my camera,
of the expression of the great mechanist of antiquity - Give me a fulcrum for my
lever, and I will move the world. Oh what pictures we would make, if we could
command our points of view!

The frustrations that Frith had to endure were evidently the common lot of the photographers of his
generation; for his contemporary, JWG Gutch, in trying to capture the sublime scenery of the Lake
District, expressed himself in phrases that virtually echoed those of Frith:

That the tourist meets with many a striking and eligible bit of scenery… well
calculated to the photographer, I will not deny, but I think it is better fitted to
the brush and painter; the distances are too great, the pictures too large, and the
aerial perspective… unattainable in photography.[88]

The better to make his case, Frith indulges in a considerable degree of overstatement; for the
foregrounds of his compositions, as those of other photographers confronted by similar problems,
were more often than not integral to the construction of the picture; for example, where the receding
lines of a road or a building might be used to lead the eye into the picture. However, a scan of a range
images of the period certainly reveals a notable proportion where the main subject appears as a
centralised mass, isolated between empty foreground and featureless sky.[i]

Frith also found the rubble strewn across many of the sites irksome. These ruins now seem to us to be
full of interest and information, evidence of how the sites appeared in the mid-nineteenth century;
but Frith saw them as an unwelcome embellishment of his pictures:

---

[i] Exposing in order to enregister natural or manmade topographical features correctly meant, within the normal range
of full daylight, simultaneously so overexposing the sky, that clouds failed to register as tones separate from the sky itself.
One possible solution was to print-in clouds from a separate negative—see appendix, *Gustave Le Gray and the Arrival*
of the Body of Admiral Bruat.

The Memnonium of Thebes: *David Roberts in his splendid work, has bestowed upon it a very respectable and recognisable profile, but my picture shows that the face is so mutilated as scarcely to leave a feature traceable.*

From our present point of view only about two-thirds of the height of the
columns is seen, in consequence of an immense accumulation of debris which
intervenes...

As he grumbles his way along the valley of the Nile, collodion sometimes coming to the boil in temperatures of 110° Fahrenheit, Frith awakens us to what differentiates the photographer in this situation from the painter. Roberts is a realist history painter. He suggests what once was: the majesty of ancient Eygpt at the height of its powers. Frith photographs what is: he is a modern archaeologist, examining ruins that excite our imagination, evoking for us glories long passed. Neither account can encompass the entire truth; neither is less than a truth. Of the Memnonium at Thebes, Frith writes:

My photograph gives the principle fragment of this statue as it now lies.
This fragment.... is merely the head and shoulders, which was of one
single block of syenite granite, and is computed to have weighed about
900 tons. It represented (Ramses the Great) *seated upon a throne...*
David Roberts in his splendid work, has bestowed upon it a very
respectable and recognisable profile; but my picture shows that the face
is so mutilated as scarcely to leave a feature traceable....

As regards the shattered condition of these statues, I have only to
refer to the Photograph, which will again, I fear, contradict some of
the representations of previous artists.

With all his enterprise, and the grandeur of his large-format photographs, Frith was a successful product of the entrepreneurial Victorian middle-class. He was highly competitive and his photographs were aimed at Roberts's market. His subject matter and the way he treated it derived from the same set of conventions of picturesque composition—so far as circumstances allowed—as that of Roberts, and a host of other artists then satisfying the appetites of a growing public by means of the lithograph and the rather more recent technique of steel engraving. It was the invention of electroplating in the 1830s that enabled the manufacture of plates made of copper surfaced with a microscopic layer of steel, which were capable of producing long runs of impressions without degradation of the finely-wrought lines of the original image (and ironically, it was an elaboration of the same process that would underwrite the expansion of the market for daguerreotype photographs by providing a technology for the mass manufacture of silver-faced copper plates by electroplating).

Gustave Le Gray: French army manoeuvres at Châlons, 1857.

Dating precisely from Frith's entrepreneurial initiative, photography would very quickly undermine the market for both lithographic and steel-engraved topographical subjects. One might be tempted to conclude from this that Frith employed technology to produce the kind of mechanical illustration that was so despised by Ruskin and Baudelaire, and that threatened to fulfill their dire predictions that photography would displace art. Yet of all the subjects available to the mid-Victorian photographer, the ruins of ancient Egypt were amongst the most frequently depicted, and the various photographers working in the pioneering 1850s each found a different means of overcoming the problems of translating reality into image, the extreme being seen in some of the works of JB Greene, who created a style that would today be termed minimalist, with human intervention in a landscape of flat sand under vast unsheltering skies sometimes reduced to a shadowy presence on the horizon. Greene's teacher in photography, Gustave Le Gray, took a similarly daring route when in 1857, by imperial command, on a misty plain, he photographed French army manoeuvres at Châlons. It would be hard to reconcile the extreme differences between the compositions of Frith for the one part, and Greene or Le Gray for the other, with the notion that the mechanistical nature of the photographic process overrules the creative sensibilities of the individual photographer. It was, quite clearly, at least partly out of the struggle to overcome the shortcomings of an emergent technology that the aesthetics of photography were constructed.

The difficulties confronting most photographers, Craven included, may have been lesser in scale than those of Frith in Egypt (whose accomplishments, incidentally, far exceeded what might have been expected from a reading of his narrative) but they were of the same technical kind. Yet in one very important respect Craven's van-camera differed from most other cameras. Its normal eyeline was raised considerably above that of cameras seated on conventional platforms. This will have helped in overcoming what Frith described as the problem of *the falling away of the ground*. When centred on the plate, the camera lens will naturally see as much below its own optical axis as above it. Thus, if the camera at ground level is set up to see (without being tilted) the top of a tall object—a tree or a building—or is far enough back to encompass a wide view, it will under normal circumstances include a great deal of foreground which may not be required, and may indeed be largely detrimental to the composition. Furthermore, with the shallow foreground depth of field[i] offered by a lens of long focal length this foreground would generally be out of focus in some degree. Frequently unavoidable as these problems were, they innocently helped to create willy-nilly a new kind of pictorial effect that some photographers successfully exploited, and which was foreign to drawing and painting—for it is

---

[i] Depth of field is the distance before or beyond the central point of focus that may still be considered as being in acceptably sharp focus.

hard to conceive of the idea of an 'out of focus' drawing; and neither was there any general convention at that era for 'empty' foreground spaces in painting. If, for its effect, much of mid-twentieth century photography would depend, in Cartier-Bresson's famous phrase, on 'the decisive moment', much of that of the mid-nineteenth would depend on 'the decisive point of view'.

Most surviving photographs from the 1850s represent only the final goal of their creators. In the case of William Craven, however, for reasons of chance or sentiment, the folios have preserved a number of rare and precious fragments that illuminate the voyage of exploration that each and every photographer of the period would have been obliged to undertake to emerge, by whatever token, master of the medium; for even those who finally proved to be the most skilled began from a very low threshold of knowledge. There were no precedents to go by. Thus, those of Craven's unfinished works that have survived offer an exceptional insight of the kind that is copiously available in the preliminary sketches, working drawings and notebooks of artists, and often now—with the benefit of X-ray technology—the actual groundwork and construction of paintings.

Convalescent and deprived of his normal winter activities—riding with the Atherstone Hunt, established in 1815 and covering an area of some four hundred square miles where Warwickshire, Leicestershire and Staffordshire conjoin; shooting pheasant at Ashdown and grouse on the Yorkshire moors; or deer stalking in Scotland—a frustrated Craven turns all his pent-up energies to exploring photography further and expanding his repertoire (as well as overseeing the reconstruction of the gardens at Ashdown, as we shall see). The folios and the album contain a record of some of the avenues opened up by Craven in the course of his solitary journeyings into photography.

A reconstruction:

Quercus petraea—the Sessile Oak—one of the common English oaks and a tree of great nobility, becomes quite literally the first focus of Craven's attention. The specimen Craven chooses as his subject should have grown straight and tall, to a hundred feet or more, living perhaps for a millenium. Although it is now devoid of neighbours it was overshadowed in its youth and grew deformed, bending towards the light, where it then found it. The photographs may presage the final days of the oak, ending them in the cull that has begun in the autumn of 1854.

Consciously or otherwise, Craven conceives the images of many of his trees in the same light as the human figure, and accordingly represents them in vertical compositions. Above half of his trees—twenty-five out of forty individuals or family groups—are portrayed so. By comparison, of Gustave Le Gray's documented total of around thirty tree subjects, varying from those barely comparable to a number very similar to Craven's, only three are in vertical format. Most photographers of the 1850s made tree images, but few were quite so dedicated to trees as were Craven and Le Gray.

As Craven observes the oak on the focusing screen with the camera-mobile levelled and the lens centred (to the photographer the image will appear inverted and laterally reversed by the lens) he is confronted by Frith's problem: the top of the tree will be cut off at the edge of the plate and there is a large unwanted area of grass too close to the camera to be within the field of sharp focus. We may speculate that for the first time in his experience Craven, while aligning the camera, is directly confronted with a practical problem of perspective: if the camera is tilted upwards to encompass the top of the tree distortion will result—the furthest part from the camera registering as smaller than the closer. If he were focused on a building the distortion would be yet more obvious, any vertical parallels appearing convergent. Buildings that are apparently leaning backwards and have converging verticals are a phenomenon familiar to anyone who has ever used an ordinary camera. It is not what we perceive if we look at the same view with our own eyes. The brain provides us with the means to make a compensatory adjustment based on experience. Like many another key problem in photography, this one of 'correct' perspective, or indeed whether it was necessary or desirable to correct perspective, was raised early in the history of photography. Schaaf quotes an exchange of letters between Sir John Herschel and Talbot, in which Herschel warns Talbot that,

Craven's first view of the tree (digital reconstruction).

> *In looking at photographic pictures from Nature.... they are hardly one in fifty perspective representations on a vertical plane. In consequence perpendicular lines all condense upwards or downwards which is a great pity.... When a high station can be chosen this is not the case and this is a reason for chusing a station half way up to the height of the principal object to be represented. Talbot promised to: always endeavour if I can to do what you recommend, place the instrument on a level with the central part of the object, or the first or second story of the building. It is however a pity that artists should object to the convergence of vertical parallel lines, since it is founded in nature and only violates the conventional rules of Art.*[89]

Tilting the camera creates distortion (digital reconstruction)

133

Here again we encounter the conflict between science and art. Talbot is on the side of art, pleading for freedom of interpretation (the camera refuses to see according to a set of preordained artificial rules) while Herschel the scientist is making the case for what is diagramatic and mechanical. Herschel would have been conscious of the potential problem even without reference to photographs, since for a long time before the invention of photography he had made extensive use—as had Talbot—of the camera lucida, an optical device that interposes a virtual image of the subject being drawn between the artist and the sheet of paper he is drawing on, aiding the assessment of mathematically correct perspective, without resorting to squaring up the paper. For the photographer, in the long term, the impossibility of always achieving an ideal viewpoint settled the matter in a practical fashion. As with unresolved foreground areas, untrue perpendiculars became—where geometrically correct perpendiculars were unattainable—a part of that language of photography that initially differentiated it from painting. Yet, in time, this alternative viewpoint—denied, in all of art, only by the perspective inventions of the Renaissance—would be absorbed into a freer vocabulary of painting, since, in any event, all two-dimensional representations of space boil down to the acceptance of a convention of seeing. In the meantime, Craven sought to represent his tree in its correct proportions by using a recently introduced piece of camera technology: the rising front. Horne and Thornthwaite's *Guide to Photography* recommended a camera that appeared to follow Frederick Scott Archer's design precisely (though without acknowledging him[i]) extolling as one of it features the rising front. This was intended to displace the image in the vertical plane whilst retaining the relative parallels of subject and plate, thus:

Count Olympe Aguado: Gros Chêne au bois de Boulogne.

> *The front of the camera holding the lens has a vertical adjustment, which enables the relative proportion of the foreground, or sky, in the required picture, to be altered without disturbing the position of the camera.*[90]

While the cross front similarly allows for lateral displacement, in this case it is the vertical adjustment of the lens that is critical in avoiding contravening the conventional rules that had governed the representation of perspective in drawing since the time of the Renaissance: perpendiculars should appear perpendicular. Craven's collection of the work of his contemporaries contained a portrait of a winter oak in the Bois de Boulogne (the print is titled in pencil *Gros Chêne au bois de Boulogne*) by Count Olympe Aguado. Close to the tree, but endeavouring to include as much of it as possible whilst reducing the foreground, Aguado has tilted the camera enough to create noticeable distortion. The perpendiculars of a building on a relative scale would have appeared to be converging markedly.

---

[i] It may be recalled that Archer recommended the company to a pupil as suppliers of chemicals.

134

To avoid this kind of distortion whilst encompassing the full height of the tree and eliminating the unwanted area of grass in the foreground, Craven determines to employ the rising front—if he is working with the camera-mobile—or, if the van-camera, the equal and opposite, that is, lowering the position of the easel that carries the plate.[i] In the dim English winter light the image projected on to the ground-glass focusing screen, even at full aperture, will appear very faint, and as, additionally, in any uncorrected lens the illumination falls off rapidly towards the edges of the lens (the review of the Plagniol lens at the Great Exhibition notes that, *the clear space which <u>all</u> the object glass illumines scarcely exceeds 6½ inches in the centre of the picture; at the edges and corners the defalcation of light is very great*). Craven fails to notice that he has exceeded necessity in elevating the lens panel (or lowering the easel) and that the image now falls partly outside the circle of illumination of the lens. That is, the top of his tree has now been cut off by the curvature of the perimeter of the lens (which will further contract as he reduces the aperture) which appears in shot as an out-of-focus soft-edged arc. As soon as he has printed the negative Craven understands the nature of his error. In a second print he tries masking the problem with card roughly cut into a matching arch. It is clearly not intended as a finished work, but an indication of whether there is a possible solution in this direction. There is not; the result is extremely inelegant.

Craven resolves the problem by returning the lens back in the direction of its central axis relative to the plate. A further plate is exposed. It is perfect. Or, less heroically but more probably, a succession of exposures accompanied by minute adjustments will have been required before the problem is resolved. We have no way of knowing, of course, how many attempts were discarded. However, this is not an error that Craven will repeat, though we can now see that the rounded shoulders of some of his subsequent prints (and those of his co-workers) were first and foremost functional, a compromise

---

[i] It may be recalled that 'Bombardier' described the van-camera, 'Grandpapa's Kodak' as having 'a stand or easel' to carry the plate.

intended to hide image cut-off where it was unavoidable. In origin, at least, arched tops to prints are not decorative, as might be supposed, though they would quickly come to be used decoratively, too. Above all, this rare sequence of images demonstrates how, in the most practical sense, photographers learned their craft, and how close to the limits of technical possibilities they worked.

Craven's trees are distinctive. Not only does he make use of the height of the van and the rising front or easel to help maintain correct proportions, but certainly in some of the images of later that winter, when the snow lies on the ground, and of the following summer of 1855, the perspective indicates that he has retreated a sufficient distance from his tree subjects to employ the lens that had been computed to cover the maximum 24-inch (60cm.) format of his camera, instead as a long focus lens, on the masked-down lesser format of 16x12-inch (40x30cm.) thus enhancing his ability to encompass the full imposing height of his trees without distortion. A further effect will be to tighten framing overall and condense foreground in particular, giving his images a characteristically concentrated look.

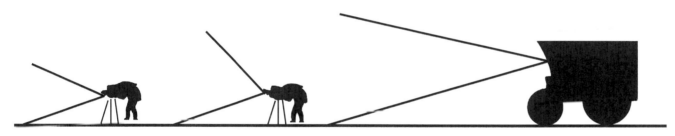

(Illustration not to scale)

Camera level, top of the tree is cut off, but image is free of distortion

Camera tilted: more tree but it is distorted

Craven's solution: elevated viewpoint, long focus lens, rising front/easel lowered. Result: full height tree, reduced foreground, correct proportions

The usual aim of Craven's contemporaries—to obtain an image that was overall sharp from the point closest to the camera to the horizon—tended to be frustrated by the optical properties of the lens: depth of field is a corollary function of aperture and focal length. It is indicative of Craven's innovative approach, and of his determination to obtain mastery of his chosen medium, that he seeks to make a virtue of this phenomenon. The fated Sessile Oak, Craven's tree of knowledge, is the subject of a further pair of comparative images, of which the first takes a relatively conventional approach to composition. The second image is startlingly offbeat. The main subject is thrust to the extreme right, its mass balanced by the lesser one of the tree located at the top left of frame (—compare this with balancing dark masses in the image of the fishermen). Most remarkably, the point of focus has been brought forward, so that no part of the image beyond the path that splits the composition is within the zone of focus. Craven has deliberately—and daringly—created an image of which a central feature is a dramatic use of differential focus. Noting the difference in distance between the oak and the tree immediately to its left, we can see that the viewpoint appears to have moved very slightly to the left, but it has not moved towards or away from the subject. The difference in framing between the two photographs, their respective zones of focus and image size, has been created by the use of two different lenses: the standard lens for 16x12 format, which will be something over 20-inches (50cm.) in the first, wider image; and the 30-inch plus (75cm.) lens employed as a long focus lens in the second image. The latter is the lens initially designed to cover the 24-inch format, as previously noted.

In this pair of images Craven takes the further step, extremely unusual at this period, of seeking to discover a totally new composition within the negative by cropping the print rather than printing the image as it has been composed on the camera's focusing screen.[i] It is the beginning of an exploration of the potential of the panoramic format, which Craven could not create directly in the cameras he owned. It will achieve its extreme form in the summer of 1855, on the one hand again by cropping a larger print; and on the other by taking the then more usual route of conjoining pairs of images to constitute a panorama.

---

[i] Cropping by selecting a section of the negative for enlargement will become a usual practice only from the end of the nineteenth century, when the means become available in the form of the enlarger with electric illuminant.

The final expression of the oak, however, is an uncropped vertical, the raddled surface of the ancient bark counterbalanced by the impenetrable darkness of the larch and tempered by the softer focus of the middle ground, these several elements surrounding what can only be described as a void. It is a composition that is the absolute converse of the commonality of images created by many of Craven's contemporaries, where attention is directed towards a concentrated centralised mass. Craven may have considered himself to have failed in his purpose in this highly experimental composition, since the sharp flat light of the winter's day provides no effect of aerial perspective at the centre of the picture. It is simply empty. There is no sense of depth created by the gradual dematerialisation of the image into the distance, which occurs naturally if only marginally in a few of Craven's other photographs. There is a possibility that the source of this composition and its intent, together with several further Craven works, is to be found in the work of an artist who was a virtuoso in creating the effects of aerial perspective, and one of whose other devices was that attenuation of foreground that characterises a majority of Craven's photographs; and whose paintings, seen by Craven many years before, were now recalled to mind. The painter was the leading German Romantic, Caspar David Friedrich (1774–1840).

Ashdown,
The Winter Trees

Through the winter of 1854/5 Craven's photography took him on a voyage of Gothic darkness which ended in a lonely place of internal exile. Of all his compatriots who practised landscape photography —John Dillwyn Llewelyn, Benjamin Brecknell Turner, Henry White, Francis Bedford, Roger Fenton— only Craven did not eulogize the English countryside. Fenton's landscapes and ruined abbeys in their totality evoke that uniquely English sense of identity that flows from the land, *This precious stone set in the silver sea.... This other Eden, demi-paradise*. But Craven's work at Ashdown did not relate in any way to the English pastoral tradition, drawing closer instead to the continental school, in particular to the paintings of Caspar David Friedrich. A key work of Friedrich's, *The Stages of Life*, is also curiously echoed in a seascape of the French photographer, Gustave Le Gray. It is one of a long sequence of photographs on which he made a tentative start in December 1855,[i] and which seems to have held a particular fascination for Craven, preoccupied as they were with the very same elements that so excercised Craven's imagination: the dramatic interplay of luminosity and darkness, and in the successful portrayal of aerial perspective, which had eluded Craven in the third image of the Sessile Oak.

There is no documented evidence of a friendship, even an acquaintanceship, between Craven and Le Gray, but a common sense examination of what little is known surely puts the question beyond doubt. Craven, as has been noted, had an apartment in Paris, where he might be found often if not regularly. He would have had ample opportunity to come into contact with Le Gray in that close society, especially since in the late 1840s Le Gray taught photography to numbers of the aristocracy. It is even possible that Craven served his apprenticeship with Le Gray. Though not amongst the fifty listed students of title, Aubenas notes that *there must have been others*.[91] There is also a definite if tangential connection: one of Le Gray's students was Count Olympe Aguado, and as we have seen, Craven added one of Aguado's treescapes to his collection. Then, too, Craven had a continuing friendship throughout his adult life with Prince Louis Napoleon, later Emperor Napoleon III, to whom Le Gray was appointed imperial photographer. There are obvious implications here for possible contact between the two photographers. Furthermore, Craven was a member of the Photographic Society of London, at whose annual exhibition Le Gray's seascape *The Brig*[ii] was shown to great acclaim in

---

[i] See appendix: Gustave Le Gray and *The Arrival of the Body of Admiral Bruat*.
[ii] Also known as *Brig on the Water*.

152

January 1857. Craven acquired a print of this photograph, as well as amassing a collection of a further eight of Le Gray's seascapes. From the evidence of the identifying stamps and numbering on seven of the prints it is clear that Le Gray's seascapes were of singular importance to Craven, who did not come by them in a single burst of enthusiasm but accumulated them over a period of time.[92] The two remaining prints in this collection, *Napoleon III's Fleet Leaving Harbour* and *Mediterranean with Mt. Agde*, are unnumbered, which suggests that they may have been gifts to Craven by the photographer. According to Nadar, Le Gray was generous to a fault: *While he was at the top the excellent Le Gray.... exhausted his stock by showering free prints on all his visitors.*[93] Yet whatever sparked Craven's admiration for the work of Le Gray, the two explored the drama of the dark image with different motives and by different methods. Craven was an amateur, unsure of himself as an artist—certainly at the outset, practical but untrained, an empiricist, and propelled by a complex of subjective feelings and emotions engendered by tradition, his love of family, and above all his new found sense of vulnerability; for this was the man who had earlier entered the lists at the Eglinton Tournament a lion, undaunted by the trial of strength and skill at arms. Le Gray, by contrast, was a professionally trained artist who was educated in the history, techniques and science of painting. He understood the theoretical background against which he set his goals. Impassioned by photography, he discovered a vocation: to expand the horizons of his adopted medium, and to prove it able to equal the glories of painting. It was to this end that he conducted his experiments in sea and cloudscape.

In a significant number of these seascapes Le Gray took the photographically radical step of pointing his lens directly towards the sun, mindful perhaps of the golden light that irradiates some of the middle-period paintings of the seventeenth century artist, Claude Lorrain, not to say those, closer to Le Gray's time, of JMW Turner, if not Caspar David Friedrich. Given that photographic printing paper is able to register a lesser range of intermediate tones than the negative from which it derives its image, and in the case of the seascapes this in turn would have been less than that of the original subject matter, it follows that by exposing the negative for the highlights and then printing these to the optimum white of the paper the darker areas will be commensurately suppressed, the lesser intermediate tones being crushed into the black, creating fiercely dramatic effects of contrast.[i] That is to say, since the printing paper cannot register the full range of contrast of the subject matter, nor its full tonal range either, one end or other of the range has to be sacrificed. In the seascapes with clouds Le Gray turned these limitations to his advantage.

---

[i] The fact that Le Gray made some seascapes using a single negative for sky and sea, and others by combine printing of a seascape with a separate cloudscape negative, does not prejudice the point made here.

Gustave Le Gray: The Brig

When the first result of this technique, the picture entitled *The Brig*, was exhibited in England it created a certain amount of confusion amongst critics and public alike. It was widely taken for a moonscape—though not by experienced photographers, who knew such a technical feat to be impossible. But given an audience familiar with the moon as a key motif in the poetry, literature and paintings of the Romantic movement, the error amongst the uninitiated was not entirely surprising. One can well imagine Craven, who had been grappling with his own ideas about the dramatic use of darkness in his photographs, being drawn to Le Gray's work—when eventually he came to see it. However, Craven's serial acquisition of Le Gray seascapes was an sign of his admiration for them rather than an acknowledgement of influence, since Le Gray executed the first of his seascapes in December 1855, after the end of Craven's most fertile year of photography, and he exhibited *The Brig*—possibly the second of his seascapes—towards the end of 1856,[i] by which time Craven had almost certainly completed his parterre series (the account of which will follow). It is even possible that what first drew Craven to Le Gray's seascapes was the paintings of Friedrich.

Caspar David Friedrich:
The Stages of Life, c.1835.

How Le Gray's *Napoleon III's Fleet leaving the Port of Le Havre* (undated) one of the photographs in the Craven collection, came to resemble so closely in form *The Stages of Life* (1834-5) by Caspar David Friedrich, seems inexplicable except as coincidence. The painting was not shown in France, and there is no record of an engraving from it that might have been seen by Le Gray. And whilst drawing out the question of the particular into the wider one about the communication of ideas between photography and painting, which, as he says, may never be answerable, Barthélémy Jobert scrupulously avoids the temptation to discover a spurious causal connection between the photograph and the painting which preceded it.[94] Yet the odds against the coincidence of imagery may not be as extreme as might at first sight appear. The painter and the photographer moved within the gravitational orbit of Romanticism, and the coincidence of the images becomes less testing when one considers that the essence of both images lies in the sentiments that widely inhabited the heart of Romanticism: the sea as a symbol of separation, and the sense of yearning, darkness and death that suffuse both pictures, which also project a feeling of unease, of a narrative unexplained, an ending unresolved. Nor was it the unlikely coincidence of two isolated images; for Friederich painted a score and more of canvases that featured seascapes and Le Gray took over forty seascape photographs. What bound Craven to Friedrich, however, is more easily explained, since it is entirely possible that there was an actual connection between the vision realised in Craven's photographs and the paintings of Caspar David Friedrich.

Gustave Le Gray: Napoleon III's
fleet leaving the port of Le Havre.

---

[i] That is, prior to exhibition at the Photographic Society. See: Jacobson, *The Lovely Sea View.*

155

Caspar David Friedrich:
Tree with Crows.

Caspar David Friedrich:
The Chasseur in the Forest.

Caspar David Friedrich:
The Chalk Cliffs on Rügen.

Craven set out on his Grand Tour a few years after his father's death, taking a route that would lead him through Northern and Central Europe and Russia, inspired by the memory of youthful readings of his grandmother's accounts of her travels. Only briefly on that trip did Craven finally pass through Northern Italy (taking ship from Trieste to Venice, thence home through France) where he might have encountered other more conventional tourists of his own elevated class. In Hayter's portrait, the twenty-two year old Craven projects the image of every fashionable rebel seeking to escape the ordinary and the predictable. Yet beyond his outward appearance Craven takes no inspiration from the English Romantic poets; he has no taste for a life of dissipation in Italy nor for Greek wars. Craven at this age weaves his own fantasies—he has an ancestor who was the champion of the Winter Queen and by some accounts her lover; a grandmother who, in the final years before the French Revolution, was welcomed by Marie-Antoinette to the court of Versailles; was an intimate of Catharine the Great, Empress of Russia; became the paramour of a German prince; and died in exile with the title of Princess of the Holy Roman Empire. All Craven's instincts directed him towards the North, not to the Mediterranean. Given his social standing and memories of his grandmother Craven, too, was naturally invited to visit the courts of the rulers of the states through which he travelled. These included Prussia and Russia, where the Crown Prince Friedrich Wilhelm and Czar Nicolas I respectively were patrons of Caspar David Friedrich as well as other artists associated with the German Romantic movement. It might readily be supposed that Craven met with the work of Friedrich in the courts of these two potentates. It is equally possible that Craven visited Friedrich in Dresden, which was on his itinerary, and perhaps even purchased sketches or drawings from him. In his penetrating and moving study of Friedrich's life and work William Vaughan notes, apropos of a possible visit to Friedrich's studio by JMW Turner in 1835, that *in his letters at this time Friedrich frequently reported foreign - including English - visitors to his studio,*[95] and as Emily Mary's later travel diaries attest on numerous occasions, reporting frequent visits to all the important art galleries of Europe, the Cravens maintained a lifelong interest in painting.

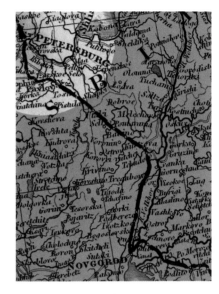

Craven marked his route on a set of Arrowsmith maps. St Petersburg is seen above, Dresden below.

Craven will encounter the work of Caspar David Friedrich at a highly impressionable age. He is barely twenty, and it will have a lasting effect on him. The later echo of Friedrich's paintings in Craven's photographs is too frequent and too precisely referential to be no more than coincidence. There is nothing in Craven's very traditional English aristocratic background, his upbringing in the Anglican church, or his later life—so far as it may be known—to suggest that he might have taken the smallest interest in the mystical Christian vision that lay at the heart of Friedrich's painting. Yet the mood and the formal qualities, including the detailed and naturalistic portrayal of nature, may well have struck

a deep chord in Craven that remained buried until it resurfaced late in 1854. *These are reveries, dreams, visions in sleep and in the night.... Friedrich himself said that he could not explain, but that each should find his own meaning in another's image.*[96] Craven's beloved trees, seen through the lens of his camera, in the darkness of winter, powerfully evoke Caspar David Friedrich's imagery; and struck down untimely at the age of forty-five Craven was perhaps reminded that Friedrich too, in his prime, had suffered the first of a series of strokes which eventually put an end to his life as a painter. In the winter tree images Craven's work takes on a new bleak aspect, entirely remote from the joys of the previous summer's photographs of his children.

Craven's treescapes are touched by that quality that is expressed in the phrase that the French sculptor, David d'Angers, used in reference to Friedrich—*the tragedy of landscape.* Many of Le Gray's trees have the light dancing behind them. Even in the Bois de Boulogne, on the edge of Paris, the light seems to come from the far South, from the Mediterranean. Fenton's softly wooded English hills, in turn, are covered with sunlit trees that are heavy and fecund. But like Friedrich's, Craven's is the brooding, melancholy landscape of Northern Europe, represented in deep saturated hues, even in images of summer.

The story of art is, by one measure, that of the influence of artist upon artist. Craven did not imitate Friedrich's work, he drew upon it, he found enlightenment in it. It provided him with a key with which to access his own deeper sentiments. But the figure that is an inevitable part of almost every Friedrich painting, most frequently seen from the rear, contemplating the same landscape as that which the artist is painting, the human being facing the vastness of Nature and the unknowableness of God, which can only be mediated by Christ, is nowhere to be seen in Craven's photographs. Craven is not creating symbolic, mystical tableaux, nor is he meditating on the sublime; he is confronting his own inner thoughts. The camera is Craven in these landscape photographs; it is the ego—*ich*—the essence of the man, contemplating the trees.

The climax of Craven's tree sequence is achieved in the stark, reductive, isolated image of the base of another ancient oak (which he has rendered more emphatic by eliminating the background) that stands as the substitute for Friedrich's Gothic cathedrals. It is a tree that owned the piece of earth it stood on long before Ashdown was built. This was no decaying stump to be uprooted and discarded. It is no more likely that this ancient relic would be destroyed by Craven in the replanting of the gardens at Ashdown, than that the Church would scatter the stones of a ruined house of God. In the language of the woodsman the tree is not dead, it is sleeping. Such an oak may take two hundred years to return to the soil, and during this time it will give sustenance to other life-forms: fern, fungus, flower, bird and insect. It will itself be responsible for its own immortality.

It is the spring of 1855. The scales have long since fallen from the eyes of those who had earlier applauded the Crimean adventure. In April, as the war enters its second year, Napoleon III and the Empress Eugénie pay a state visit to England in order to cement the Anglo-French alliance. Kate Clarendon writes in her diary:

16th April 1855

We heard today that the bombardment of Sebastopol had begun whilst we are –
in the midst of pomp and grandeur, what suffering and horrors may be going on!!! - [97]

At Ashdown, remote from the noise of war, Wild Darrell is in his last weeks of training for the Derby. In parallel with his work on the tree photographs, Craven begins to record the creation of Nesfield's parterre and, once again, we have a demonstration of the originality of his thinking. It is clear that, from the start, Craven's intention was to create a sequence in time—we have already seen how the area to be redeveloped was photographed from the lantern at the top of the house in the summer of 1854, showing its location in relation to the avenue of trees beyond. Yet, equally clearly, Craven was not interested in simply creating a didactic series, a catalogue of the work in hand. What emerges is idiosyncratic, interpretive, a unique exploration of mood and form, a meditation bounded by the passage of time.

160

The Parterre

From the parkland, looking at the corner of Ashdown House that point towards the south-west, Craven takes the first of what will become a matching pair of narrative photographs. The last of the snow is almost gone but the trees are still bare of leaves. In the foreground of the first of the time-lapse photographs Craven has purposefully included a number of garden tools leaning on some wicker fencing panels, suggesting that work on the parterre has been resumed. In the middle distance, the young yew shoots that were transplanted twelve months earlier from the nursery, where they were protected from cold winds of the Berkshire Downs—as witness the blurred fringes of the trees—are neatly silhouetted against the creamy walls of the house and the outbuildings, bordering the area of the parterre. Just behind the fencing panels in the foreground of the earlier image, and seen more clearly in the later one, is further evidence of Craven's interest in the practical. The area immediately around the house is protected from cattle grazing in the parkland beyond by wire fencing—a product still relatively new to the market. The innovation that made this possible was the process of galvanisation, providing a microscopically thin coating, but sufficient to prevent the underlying metal from rusting. Several manufacturers at the Great Exhibition were awarded prize medals for new galvanic processes using zinc, tin or lead as a protective coating on iron and copper wire ropes and sheet metal. Galvanisation was the next process in the logical line of development from electroplating, which had made the mass production of daguerreotype plates viable a decade or so earlier.

The plant nursery, with more wicker panels protecting its population of vulnerable shoots from inclement weather and the ravages of the rabbit population, is the subject of the chimney-stacked side view of the house, whose composition we have earlier related to the first group portrait of the Craven brood. It is one of two dramatic portraits of Ashdown that are part of the chronology defined by the pair of matched views, the other being a closer view of the south-east corner of the house.

164

The designer of the parterre, William Andrews Nesfield, favoured Italianate design. The parterre would be composed of intricate patterns of coloured gravels made from the likes of crushed yellow and red brick, and blue Welsh slate, laid within borders of dwarf box and beds of miniature shrubs, and incorporating fragments of coloured glass. The style was meant to replicate the ribbon patterns seen in the marble floors of many medieval Italian churches, abstract patterns of a kind that probably originated in Rome in the Middle Ages, where scattered shards and the fragments of the stone buildings of antiquity were in plentiful supply, and came to be used for decorative flooring. Not strictly part of the Gothic style, this kind of pattern was incorporated with enthusiasm into the vernacular of the neo-Gothic. In the lower right hand corner of the photograph we see heaps of coloured gravels lying ready for use. But this is no documentary photograph. With an image created by a camera positioned at near ground-level, and consummated in a print of extreme tonal contrasts, Craven turns his back on photographic realism. This is a Synthetist image, in which Ashdown begins to take on the dark aspects of an illustration for a Gothic novel, a feeling redeemed only by the refined and lively surface of the albumen print; as a drawing or an engraving it would have appeared sinister indeed.

With high summer comes Craven's apotheosis as a photographer. Work on the parterre is complete. Before the beds are planted Craven sites his camera overlooking the parterre from the first floor of the house—calculated from the angle of view—and makes two exposures, either from the extreme left and right corners of the small balcony, or from the inner corners of the adjacent windows. The fields of view of the two resulting negatives overlap. Craven trims the prints from these negatives to eliminate the overlap, and mounts them edge to edge to conjoin them into the ideal format to encompass the intricate design. The high-angle view reveals, in differential tones of grey, how the photographic emulsion has interpreted the multi-hued materials layed down in the parterre. It is a photograph of daring originality, abstracting the decorative geometry of the design from its natural surroundings. Even so, Craven's judgement—or his courage—deserts him momentarily: The power of the image is somewhat impaired by the inclusion of the putti, which look strangely out of place.

165

The beds are being planted. Craven continues his exploration of the parterre, as might a composer elaborating a theme with variations. At ground level, he creates images of the two most obvious views—from and towards the house. But his compositional skills are now highly-developed; he has acquired total confidence in the handling of camera and lenses; and he has an unerring sense of 'the decisive point of view'. Thus, the resulting images, which could easily have been no more than ordinary, fill the frame to bursting point, and convey surely the realisation of Nesfield's intent—of balance and symmetry; of embracing, in the one direction, the house within the widening spaces of the garden, and in the opposing view, projecting the house into the garden and thence through the funnel of trees, into the landscape beyond.

170

Craven envisions additional variations and the camera (not too heavy when detached from its chariot) is hauled back up to the balcony that overlooks the newly completed parterre. There, by the simple act of emloying the camera to take alternately horizontal and vertical formats, he creates two further masterworks from the identical point of view. The photographs are taken during the long twilights of summer, which renders saturated negatives emphasizing contrast at the expense of intermediate tones. The scene is transformed, now at the very edge of what may be perceived with the naked eye unaided. The first exposure is a study of pure form, expressing the essence of the parterre's design.

Then, in the wider landscape that incorporates the avenue, we drift into a world of dreams. The trees of the avenue and lawn between them possess no light of their own, and therefore reflect none; and the photographic emulsion—insensitive to some colours of the spectrum—interprets their intense green as an impenetrable black backdrop to the luminosity of the patterned foreground. The tiny, remote, seated figure of the woman in white, located eccentrically, serves only to underline the otherwise perfect symmetry of the landscape and of the photograph in which it is framed. The figure is disturbing, enigmatic, it upsets our automatic assumptions about scale. The photograph objectivizes an extreme subjective point of view, that of an eye seeing a model at table-top level in which the foreground looms unnaturally large, which is so unusual a viewpoint in terms of the everyday that the brain has no inbuilt mechanism with which to rationalise it. Thus, the parterre takes on the dimensions almost of an amphitheatre. The choice of viewpoint and the perspective of the lens that Craven has selected for the photograph turn the world topsy-turvy.

What a curious feeling! said Alice; I must be shutting up like a telescope.

And so it was indeed: she was now only ten inches high, and her face brightened up at the thought that she was now the right size for going though the little door into that lovely garden.[98]

171

Family Affairs

Kate, the Countess of Clarendon, is one of the foremost political hostesses of her day, her diaries endlessly listing the guests—sometimes running into dozens—at dinner parties given twice a week or more at the Clarendons' family home, The Grove, in Hertfordshire, within easy reach of London; or else at their Mayfair house in Grosvenor Crescent. But though the Cravens have no involvement in affairs of state, Kate does not neglect the sister she loves. Clarendon was appointed Foreign Secretary in 1853, and was of necessity in touch almost daily with Queen Victoria and Prince Albert during the critical period of the war in the Crimea, and Kate's contact with Emily Mary and her family—the girls in particular, whom Kate loved dearly—seems to offer her a measure of respite from the pressures generated by her husband's responsibilities, and from the stresses of grand occasions, which frequently involve Kate playing hostess to the royal couple.

On 23rd July 1855, Kate notes, with evident pleasure:

> I _think_ it was this day that we had a small but _very_ pleasant dinner - Lord
> Lansdowne, the Cravens and Elizabeth Craven, Dowr. Lady Mosley,
> Villiers, Lister, Corry Courcellan and ourselves - it was more like a chatty
> dinner in a country home than a London dinner.[99]

The occasional lapse of memory when it came to dates and even the names of the less prominent among her guests is forgivable. The demands of diplomacy and the London season were enough to test the toughest of constitutions. Six weeks before the dinner party, Kate writes:

> I took Bettine Craven under my chaperonage tonight to Lady Londesborough's
> ball and stayed till about 3 o'clock in the morning her Mama having been all
> day at Eton and herself too, but the young Lady did not consider that fatigue
> sufficient to make her give up the ball, so I chaperoned.[100]

174

In August, Queen Victoria and Prince Albert payed a return visit to Napoleon III and the Empress Eugénie. It was an occasion ruled by formality and high protocol, and Kate, though a familiar in court circles, was not included in the Queen's party. At liberty for once, she seized the opportunity to visit Ashdown:[i]

Tues 21st Aug 1855

The three girls and I went up to London by the early Train in order to go and see Mrs George who was not quite well, before we started for Ashdowne - we arrived at Shrivenham where Emily Craven with carriages &c was ready to convey us and our luggage to Ashdowne - a lovely afternoon - I had not seen Ashdowne since the alterations and additions and immensely improved I thought it, tho' always a delightful quaint old place - the blowing air of those downs too so fresh wholesome and invigorating.[101]

And then comes the most enchanting of testimonials:

Wedn 22nd August 1855

I am much bit with Craven's photographing - it is beautiful.

Tues 28th August 1855

We left Ashdowne after a very pleasant visit of a week - Emily Craven so dear and affectionate and Craven as he always is all kindness - our mutual children so happy and merry together - then we sketched, drove, walked, photographed &c &c together - the air was so pure and bracing and the change from ones usual ways very good for us I am sure.[102]

---

[i] Which she constantly misspells.

Kate's choice of phrase—*photographed.... together*—seems to indicate that she sees herself as an active participant, if not in the photography of the landscape, then at least in the photographs of her daughters, and the evocation of herself in the company of Emily Mary, reading, writing, relaxing on a summer's afternoon in the quiet calm of the drawing-room at Ashdown. The camera's low angle engenders a sense of intimacy; the mirror, endlessly reflecting a complimentary one opposite, lends a sense of timelessness; while as a backdrop, the white muslin drapes (protecting furniture and fabrics from fading in the sunlight) float like the benign disembodied spirits of Cravens past.

The previous day, Kate's husband George had written to her—as he did most days they were apart— telling her, to her relief, of the successful completion of the royal visit, and reassuring her that the party were all safe. Not long before, an attempt had been made on the life of Napoleon III.

> *So that wonderful and important visit to Paris is over!! and over in safety*
> *and without an accident - how thankful we ought to be!! for what a number of*
> *dreadful things might have taken place!!!*[103]

Emily Mary and her third daughter Blanche, in need of dentistry, followed Kate back to London. George Johnstone, the younger of the fourteen-year-old twins belonging to Craven's sister, Louisa, joined his aunts and cousin for lunch at Grosvenor Crescent. At that very moment, through no fault of this young man, the Johnstone inheritance was in the process of creating a great deal of turbulence within the Craven family.

By the mid-nineteenth century, the ties that bound the Cravens to the Berkeleys and the Clarendons went back two centuries, and give some indication of how closely interwoven were the interests of the most powerful families in the kingdom. John, Lord Berkeley, Sir William Berkeley, The Earl of Clarendon, and Sir William Craven had all been amongst the supporters of Charles I and then of his exiled son. At the restoration of the Stuart monarchy in 1660, the latter, crowned Charles II, rewarded the faithful with grants of vast tracts of largely unsettled land in Virginia and North Carolina, which had been under British colonial rule since the time of Queen Elizabeth I. The recipients of this largess were known as the Lords Proprietors. No surviving documentation indicates that successive Lords Craven did anything by way of developing or otherwise exploiting these assets beyond selling off parcels of land from time to time. In 1856, the Craven holdings in the residual areas of this territory were stated to be: *560,509 acres of land of the 1st 2nd and 3rd class and 147,000 acres of refuse land.* Its realisable value earlier in the century must have been negligible, or Craven's father would surely have disposed of it to relieve the mortgages on his English properties, or Craven himself would have done so to help amortize the debts he inherited.

The Johnstone family acquired their American land interests much later than the Cravens. Louisa Craven's husband inherited from his father, who in turn inherited from his uncle, Sir William Johnstone Pulteney, who had made the large part of his vast fortune in India in the latter part of the eighteenth century. As a speculation, Pulteney purchased 46,000 acres of wilderness in the State of New York after the American War of Independence, but like the Cravens' American land holdings, this continued largely unsettled at mid-nineteenth century.

Louisa's marriage to Sir George Johnstone—who, we recall, was one of Craven's valiant companions at the Eglinton Tournament—was short-lived. Wedded on 24th October 1840, George died on 7th May 1841, having fallen from his horse while out hunting. He left Louisa pregnant with twins. Either after their birth, or after Louisa remarried in 1844, her brother—the photographer's youngest brother—the Hon. Frederick Keppel Craven was appointed legal guardian to the boys.

A single legal document surviving in the Craven family tells us that the Craven and Johnstone assets in America were amalgamated into one trust, together with 571 tenanted dwellings in and around Weymouth, Dorset, and further more marginal assets in the Weymouth area, that had all been part of the Johnstone inheritance.[i] Both William and Frederick Craven were among the trustees. The primary object of the trust was apparently to ensure a continuing source of income for the orphaned twins— particularly important for their future security after their mother remarried and had further children. The trust's plan, perfectly sound, or so it seemed, was to encourage the settlement of vacant parcels of land it owned by providing applicants with a private mortgage, that is, one financed by the trust itself. Once established, these settlers would in turn attract others to the neighbouring areas. The price of the land to successive waves of settlers would be increased gradually, as the communities grew and became more prosperous and secure. The plan could hardly fail.

---

[i] The Dorset properties were entitled to return three members to parliament—an important source of political influence to Sir William Johnstone Pulteney, when he purchased them back in the era of 'pocket boroughs'.

Over a period of time, it became clear that sales were slower than had been hoped for, and that a canny and top-heavy administration of land-agents in America, and lawyers in England and Scotland, in a practice well-established over the centuries, were stripping much of the value out of the scheme before a penny reached the supposed beneficiaries. Matters came to a head in 1856. One faction amongst the trustees, headed by Frederick Craven—who undoubtedly took his responsibilities as guardian to the Johnstone twins very seriously—sought to replace the existing land-agents, sharply increase the price of land as yet unsold, and pursue any first settlers who might have been in arrears with their mortgage payments, though it had been a principle of the scheme in its initial stages that these people be shown, *every facility and indulgence in regard to their their payment*, in view of the fact that it was their presence that enhanced the value of adjacent plots. William Craven, on the other hand, took a less critical and perhaps less realistic view of the day-to-day administration than did his brother. The submission of the main American agent, who had much to lose, whilst providing an inflated value for the remaining land in the State of New York, backed up his argument with the plausible opinion that, *the appearance of a Stranger among the Settlers with an authority to direct a more active system of management by selling the remaining land without respect to price or gradual demand for it and a forced collection on past sales would produce great disaffection in the minds of Settlers, check the sales of remaining lands and result in great injury to the trust.* As to the fate of the unsold land in Virginia, it seemed impossible to extract any reliable information from the American agents, who offered no more than that they were about to commission a new survey of it. William Craven ought to have taken heed, but perhaps by now more careless in business matters than once he had been, and given his proven record of concern for the wellbeing of his own tenants, there can be little doubt that he found the idea of *forced collection* unsavoury, to say the least; and so, if for no other reason, he took a stand. There can be no question that the agents and lawyers were pulling the wool over his eyes.

The Johnstone twins.

While after two miserable years of war peace was finally declared in the Crimea, hostilities were about to break out on the home front. Disagreement over the running of the trust turned to anger, and Cain rose up against his brother. A court hearing ensued, with William and his advisers confronting Frederick, as appointed guardian of Frederick John William Johnstone, Bart., legally 'an infant', and his faction. The court found for neither party and left the existing administration of the trust in place, except for putting a supervisory order on its officers—doubtless to little effect. Nothing has been discovered that indicates any further resolution of the problem within the lifetime of William Craven. The court case coincided precisely with the beginning of the season in London, and in the midst of these stressful events Kate records:

The casual use of backdrops was common in early portrait photographs. In a fruitless attempt to turn this exterior into an interior Craven has also opaqued the 'floor' area.

179

Fri 9th May 1856. Went to Emily Craven's pretty ball

Fri 16th May. Dined at the Jersey's today and <u>both</u> went

afterwards to Emily Craven's second ball.[104]

The Craven daughters were growing up. Bettine was twenty, Evelyn Mary seventeen, and Blanche almost fifteen. Their passage into society was of paramount importance.

The American conflict resulted in a coolness between Craven and his brother Frederick. There would be no more fishing trips together. But worse was to follow. Already vulnerable, Craven's health failed once again. Once more there are gaps in the surviving correspondence and on this occasion Kate's diary is of no help, and so the illness goes undocumented within the family. However, Craven is recorded as having resigned the honorary post of Lord Lieutenant of Warwickshire in 1857 on grounds of ill health; and his obituary in *The Times* in 1866 noted that about eight years before his death, that is 1857 or 58, he had suffered an attack that from the correspondent's description—*a paralysis on one side*—was certainly a second stroke. Whatever the contributary causes—and the stress brought on by the Johnstone affair must be the prime suspect—Craven would never fully regain his health.

Neither would the rift between Craven and Frederick ever be completely healed. Circulating within the confines of a closed society they could not entirely avoid contact; however, Frederick kept himself as far distant as possible from his brother's family. It is more than likely than Emily Mary had expressed herself with her usual forthrightness on the subject of the trust and Frederick detested her for it, if for no better reason. Frederick had an intimate friend in the person of his first cousin, Lady Caroline Fitzhardinge Maxse, née Berkeley, whom he addressed in the most affectionate of terms; so much so that it seems likely that Frederick, a bachelor, was in love with her. He certainly withheld nothing from her. On April 3rd 1860, Frederick wrote:

My Dearest Caroline,

I have written today to Popham proposing to go over to Littlecote to look at the bay horse on

Saturday. I could not well go before as he does not deal in horses on Good Friday, and as

I could not get an answer until Thursday I will let you know my opinion of the horse

as soon afterwards as possible.... We have a most excellent account of Craven today,

he is reported to be very much better than he has been for months.[105]

180

The horse in question was Buccaneer, born in 1857, the great son of a noble father—Wild Dayrell. Buccaneer would become one of the champions of his age, winning eleven of thirteen races in which he started. Forced at last to retire due to a leg injury, he was sold by his owner, Lord Portsmouth, to the Hungarian State Stud. In the course of a lifetime he went to mares all over Europe, and sired no less than fourteen Derby winners.

A few days later Frederick wrote to his cousin again:

Many thanks for the two letters my dearest Caroline

....I am going this afternoon to see (if they will allow me) Buccaneer, our horse for the Derby. I hear that he is in first rate condition and Lord Portsmouth and many others are very sanguine about his success, they say he is to run for the 2000 gns Stakes, if he wins that we shall have much the best of our bet....

....Popham writes me word that my family will come over for the day - I could have dispensed with their presence on the occasion, but I do not suppose that we shall interfere with one another - I was sorry to hear that Mary has been playing the fool with old Tom as I had been led to imagine that she and William had been going on admirably, it would not take me long to cut my throat were I married to that Lady - I do not know when the parties could have met at Heaton [i] *- certainly Mary was in London all last week and went to Ashdown on Tuesday last....*

I can give you a very good account of myself - bless you my very dear Coz.

Your ever affec. Fredk Craven

---

[i] Heaton Hall, near Manchester, was the home of the Earl of Wilton.

Who was *old Tom?* It is difficult to believe that Emily Mary might have been guilty of anything more scandalous than attracting the unsought attentions of an admirer. Given the extraordinary vehemence with which Frederick vented his feelings about Emily Mary, it seems to have been a case of him passing on tittle-tattle, since further into the letter Frederick admits that, *I do not know when the parties could have met.... certainly Mary was in London all last week and went to Ashdown on Tuesday last where she is still staying.* But also to be taken into account is the state of Frederick's mind caused by degeneration in his health, for he was an alcoholic. After seeing his doctor he assures his cousin: *My Dearest Caroline....I will do everything in my power to return to my former health.* In this, he failed. But in an undated letter Frederick's medical attendant, one Dr Quin, aware of his closeness to his cousin, informs her of the tragic news:

> *Dear Lady Caroline*
> *Fred did everything he promised and came and spoke openly and candidly with respect to his symptoms. I was.... equally candid and telling him that there was no doubt that his complaint was DT.*[i]

*The Hon. Frederick Craven
(detail from the Fishing Party).*

On 17th June 1864, Frederick writes from his home at 14, Park Street, Grosvenor Square:

> *My Dearest Caroline,*
> *Nothing would give me so much pleasure as to see you on Monday June 27 - we must make arrangements as to time, for I see a MD every morning and will desire him to stay away.*

It was too late. Before the appointed day Caroline received a letter from William:

> *June 21 1864*
> *My dear Caroline*
> *we lost my dear Brother this morning at half past 3 oclock for the last few hours he had not the will and faded away without pain as if in sleep. I enclose here a letter which I found on his table. If I can do anything command me....*

Frederick Craven's animosity towards his sister-in-law was of long standing, dating back at least to when the fraternal conflict over the Johnstone inheritance began to come to the boil, in the summer of 1855. As Emily Mary's letters make clear, reticence was not in her nature, and she doubtless gave her husband the most vigorous support in the disagreement with Frederick. That summer, recovered—at least physically—from his stroke Craven was at the height of his creative powers as a photographer.

---

[i] Delirium Tremens, a symptom of chronic alcoholism.

182

Ashdown, 1855
THE SUMMER TREES

Though Craven would never again produce photographs quite as spellbinding as those of the parterre—his masterpieces—taken during the glorious summer of 1855, nor of the monumental base of the oak tree, his voyage of exploration in the medium was far from over.

In Craven's later work, as in much of his output, it is only by inference that we can arrive at some semblance of a chronology. Whilst a large and important quantity of family photographs were taken in 1856, it is very probable that the work continued well into 1857. Clothing and ambient light suggest summer in all of these photographs. At all events, the photographs preceded Craven's next serious bout of illness, which almost certainly occurred in the second half of 1857. Kate's diaries inform us that Emily Mary gave a ball on 1st June, at the start of that year's season. She would hardly have done so had her husband been seriously incapacitated. Kate herself gave a dinner party on 14th October following, at which Emily and Evelyn were present, but not Craven. Having fallen ill he might have appeared to be on the road to recovery, but not up to socialising. A rough assessment of the ages of the Craven children in the group of photographs would appear to corroborate the approximative dates. One deeply shocking aspect of the photographs, which include some images of Craven himself, is how much and how fast he has aged as a result of his first stroke.

When precisely these family images date from, however, is a matter of less consequence than how they interrelate. As individual or group portraits they have enchantment; in combination, they provide a further remarkable example of Craven's propensity for experimentation. Craven added dimension to his photography not by travelling the world and responding to external stimuli, but by having faith in photography's capacity to expand from within, limited only by the breadth of his own imagination.

The key image in large format is the family group, echoing the 1853 photograph of the children—the tondo—but which now includes Emily Mary and Craven himself. It is important to notice their clothing, which informs us that the two subsequent images, of Emily Mary and Craven individually, are part of the same session. For these latter images, Emily Mary is posed looking off to camera-right, that is to her left; while Craven is looking off to camera-left, that is to his right. Their eyelines match perfectly. The two images are mounted on the page so that the couple are looking at one another. To the photographs of the parterre, connected only sequentially, Craven has now added a further,

190

psychological element, describing the relationship between the couple. The terms 'camera-right', 'camera-left' and 'eyeline'—commonly used in film-making—are apposite, since Craven has effectively invented storyboarding as it would come to be used in the movies; and furthermore (mimicking in spacial arrangement what the movie film does in time) has arrived at the idea of intercutting in editing—by juxtaposing images on the page in such a way as to give superadditional meaning to the separate elements. In three 'shots' Craven gives an account of his family and his relationship with his wife after more than twenty years of marriage. Not only would a further half-century elapse before the first simple, single-take movies appeared (and even Craven, with all his ingenuity, could hardly be supposed to have predicted the invention of the movies) but it would take a further generation beyond that before the sophistication of this kind of intercutting between characters would be added to simple, narrative sequences in the movies.

Craven's sequence of shots carries such conviction that only at second glance does one register the one oddity—that Craven has used the same camera set-up, with the left-hand balustrade as seen in the family group as background—for the successive singles of Emily Mary and himself, and that—though it detracts not one wit from the effect he is seeking—the geography is therefore incorrect. The reason for this 'error' is that Craven will have sketched his wife's position on the focusing screen to enable perhaps the photographer daughter, Evelyn Mary, to match it precisely when he took up the pose. The camera itself has not been moved, thus the framing remains the same.

If it is tempting to see this notion of a pre-cinema picture-story narrative as a rather fanciful interpretation of a random idea that has worked out by chance, Craven offers us further examples of his unique space-time arrangement, achieving similar ends by slightly variant means. The most charming of these derives from an image of the two youngest girls, Beatrix Jane and Emily, sharing the pleasures of a book. Each of the girls is then reprinted as an individual close-up portrait—or 'shot' if one is to sustain the movie analogy—and they are juxtaposed on the page in such a way as to suggest a sequence in which Emily is listening to her older sister reading. The entire concept is unique to Craven.

193

Craven does not deliberately address himself to the future; he neither predicts nor prefigures; and all the indications are that, working in isolation, he contributed nothing to the general advance of the art of photography in the 1850s. Yet, with the perspective of time, we can see that his photography does foreshadow many of the most significant developments in the wider context of the art in the early part of the twentieth century. Where in his own era photography was generally attempting to extend its tonal range, Craven is deliberately and systematically making use in his imagery of extreme contrasts of a kind of that will in due course be reinvented, each in his own fashion, by Atget, Paul Strand, Ansel Adams, Bill Brandt, and their like. He uses selection and cropping to give emphatic meaning, where his contemporaries generally accept the constraints of the frame as given. Where, in Craven's time, photography stood accused of excessive and even simple-minded realism, Craven creates surrealism and plays games with perspective. He builds sequences in time and creates movie-style narrative. Above all, Craven stands at the threshold of that period in which photography begins to mature into a medium of considered individual reflection. He will be followed very shortly by Lewis Carroll, Julia Margaret Cameron, Lady Hawarden, Nadar, and their like, each one an artist with an intensely subjective vision.

It would not be long before the marital harmony implied in Craven's photographs was put to the test in a manner beyond predictability.

In November 1858, the French Emperor, Napoleon III, invited the Clarendons and the Palmerstons, together with the Cravens and a party of other friends to join him at a grand hunting party in the Forest of Compiègne, just to the North-East of Paris. The outing turned out to be little short of disastrous for almost everyone concerned. In her diary, Kate Clarendon describes the expedition only insofar as to say that the journey to Compiègne was just about tolerable and that when they arrived a programme of horseracing had to be abandoned because of the dreadful weather. In a rare act of self-censorship—presumably out of loyalty to her husband—she passes over the political row generated in Britain by the visit. Lord Palmerston's government having been out of office since being defeated in the Commons the previous February, he and Clarendon were heavily censured by the British press for accepting the Emperor's invitation. There was deep anxiety in Britain at Napoleon's ambitions to assume leadership of the Anglo-French entente. As ex-Prime Minister and ex-Foreign Secretary respectively, and with every intention of standing for office again, they appeared to be placing themselves in the dangerously ambiguous position of being not simply private guests of the Emperor but, to the suspicious, unofficial informants on British foreign policy. In his memoirs, Lord Malmesbury, a longstanding friend of both the Emperor and of Clarendon (as well as the political rival of the latter, having taken on the post of Foreign Secretary in the goverment that succeeded that of Palmerston) noted, *I hear that Lords Palmerston and Clarendon now think they have done a foolish thing by going to Compiègne.*[106] In due course the row would blow over, and Palmerson was returned to office the following year as leader of the newly formed Liberal party.[i]

As for the sport at Compiègne, Clarendon wrote to his friend Lady Manchester:

I think I left off writing to you when I was sent for to go a-gunning at Compiègne, but the chasse was given up as it was raining too hard, and the day was got through by such pastimes as a conversation spirituelle kept up by thirty people, football in the gallery and quadrilles on horseback in the manège, and the Emperor doing the lance excercise and other equestrian feats à la Franconi for the amusement of the Court. The next day was fine and we had a chasse au tire; each tireur had four guns provided for him with four loaders in cocked hats; the beaters were a squadron of lancers in boots and spurs, with a trumpeter who signified to them what they were to do. It was a pretty gay scene, but I believe that most of the creatures had been turned out the day before, or were let out of traps as the Emperor approached.[107]

Napoleon III 'photographed from life at Fontainbleu'. Photo: Thiebault, 1860s.

Some while earlier, Clarendon's wife, Kate, had painted a decidedly cool picture of their host's charms, quite apart from his thoroughly unsporting habits:

The Emperor's countenance is very curious, there is something of melancholy about it - but it strikes one also that it <u>might</u> look very <u>savage</u> - there is a want of proportion about his figure which takes much off from grace, his head and shoulder have the appearance of belonging to a much taller man than he is - his legs are much too short yet his manners are dignified from their composure, and he plays his part in the best taste, a very difficult part to play and it is admirable how he does it - he looks very well on horseback.[108]

[i] In the political horsetrading that followed, however, Clarendon lost the post of Foreign Secretary to Lord John Russell.

195

Kate had presumably not seen him unseated at the Eglinton Tournament.

The cold autumn evenings at Compiègne were given over to party games at which the Emperor was accompanied by his wife, the Empress Eugénie (according to a persistent rumour, Clarendon's illegitimate daughter) as well as his mistress, Madame Walewska, wife of a French diplomat. Naturally, Emily Mary was present. More notable for the strength of her personality than her physical beauty, then in her mid-forties and facing the inevitable prospects of middle-age and menopause, and with an intermittently ailing husband to contend with, it comes as no surprise to discover that Emily Mary was pleased as well as flattered to find herself the object of the Emperor's attentions, which were both indiscreet and unprincipled—after all, her husband was a lifetime friend of the Emperor. As the lie of the land became clear, La Walewska—with the support of the Empress, who would rather the devil she knew—began to show her animosity. On his return to England, over a lingering lunch, Clarendon regaled Lord Malmesbury with further details of the week's events:

> *Lady Mary Craven was immensely admired. The Empress and Madame Walewska*
> *were loud in their admiration of her, but towards the end of the week they had very much*
> *cooled.*[109]

There can be no doubt that Emily Mary had tripped, though there is no suggestion that she had fallen. Nevertheless—as evidenced by the inclusion of the story in two of the most important political memoirs of the day—an unpleasant if entertaining scandal was brewing within this close-knit community. Craven was having none of it. Abruptly, he quit Compiègne with Emily Mary in tow. Savouring every word (he does not sound very sympathetic towards his sister-in-law) Clarendon picks up the story:

> *In the evening we had a charade, at which 'grand presence' of Mary Craven was much*
> *wanting. She would have willingly yielded to the Imperial entreaties to stay, but*
> *Monsr. le Mari would not hear of it.* [i] *I doubt that the entreaties were backed by*
> *the Walewska, who began to think it was high time she should be off....*[110]

In the long term, any crisis of confidence that arose between Craven and his wife was overcome. Yet, it was easier for the Emperor to make mischief than for the mischief to be undone. Almost eighteen months elapsed between the events at Compiègne and Frederick Craven's letter to Lady Caroline:

---

[i] Le Mari - the husband.

196

I was sorry to hear that Mary has been playing the fool with old Tom as I had been led to imagine that she and William had been going on admirably. In view of the general formality of address in Victorian England, such a casual reference as *'old Tom'* —given that Emily Mary is hardly likely to have responded to the advances of the gardener, the coachman, or her husband's valet—would seem unusual, unless it were a nickname mutually understood between writer and recipient. There is indeed such a possibility. In 1844 the American showman, P T Barnum, brought the midget known as General Tom Thumb to Europe for the first time,. The midget was a smash hit. As well as making stage appearances before an enthusiastic public at the Egyptian Hall in London, he entertained in private in the homes of many of the nobility, and on three occasions was received in private audience by Queen Victoria, for whom he performed at Buckingham Palace. One of his favourite turns (though perhaps not before the Queen) was an impersonation of Napoleon Bonaparte, the uncle of Napoleon III. The inevitable conclusion is that Napoleon III, who might in justice himself be called a Bonapartist impersonator, one not universally admired amongst the English aristocracy and, incidentally, of no great physical stature either, as indicated by Kate Clarendon, came to be known mockingly in some circles as *'Old Tom'* — after the undersized General. For over twenty years, General Tom Thumb continued to tour in Europe under the aegis of Barnum and other promoters, and he was appearing in England, as popular as ever, at about the time of Frederick Craven's letter to Lady Caroline. Frederick Craven's mention of Heaton lends further intrigue. Heaton Hall was the home of the Earl and Countess of Wilton, who were famous for the lavishness of their entertaining. After the shortlived Italian campaign, and with the restabilisation of the Anglo-French entente, Napoleon III once again took to making private visits to England.[i] There is every reason to believe that he—*'Old Tom'* —was a guest at Heaton Hall, as implied by Frederick Craven's letter. He was certainly well acquainted with the Earl of Wilton who, in 1858, as Commodore of the Royal Yacht Squadron, had proposed the Emperor as a member of that exclusive club. And in the same year, the Cravens' eldest daughter Bettine, then aged twenty-two, had married Viscount Grey de Wilton, son of the Earl.

Old Tom' - General Tom Thumb as Napoleon Bonaparte. Half of a hand-coloured stereo card distributed by the London Stereoscopic Company, c.1860.

The tribal boundaries were very narrow, and innuendo of the kind broadcast by the ailing Frederick Craven—did Emily Mary actually visit her in-laws at Heaton while the Emperor was there? —would have been difficult to deflect.

There is a surviving note from the Emperor's residence, the Palais des Tuileries:

---

[i] After being deposed in 1870, Napoleon III and his family took refuge in England, where he died in 1874.

197

*Le Premier Chambellan prie monsieur le Comte Craven d'avoir la bonté de vouloir
bien lui faire savoir de plutôt possible si rien ne s'oppose à ce qui'il se rende à
l'invitation qu'il a l'honneur de lui faire parvenir.*

The Chief Chamberlain requests Count [i] *Craven to have the goodness to make
known to him as soon as possible if there is anything that prevents him from
responding to the invitation that he has had the honour of extending to him.*

Indeed, there was. Craven's lack of response speaks for itself: the episode was closed; the friendship at an end.

For Craven, the decade of the 1860s began with a grievous loss. His beloved mother, Louisa, died on 27th August 1860. Meanwhile, the generations succeeded one another. The Cravens' first son, William Frederick Augustus, Viscount Uffington—Uffie—who had joined the Grenadier Guards in 1858, was part of a detachment that accompanied the Prince of Wales on a visit to Canada in 1860. George, his junior by three years, joined the Scots Fusilier Guards; and twelve-year-old Osbert—Obbie— commenced his studies at Eton. Craven had at last commissioned plans from the Nesfields for the improvement and extension of Combe Abbey and the redesign of its gardens and, drawing a line under the *affaire Napoleon*, planned an extended tour of the Continent accompanied by Emily Mary. In July 1861, together with their second daughter, Evelyn Mary, they left England en route for Germany. At age twenty-two, Evelyn Mary had become, certainly by her mother's account, an able photographer, and discovered that the art could have other rather more nefarious uses than those to which Craven put it:

*A search was made for Franz to have his photograph taken, but he was not to
be found and it afterwards turned out he had gone to Darmstadt with a 'Herrschaft'.*
(The next day) *Mary and I went to see about Franz's photograph and after waiting
for a long time.... Franz with much pleasure put himself into what he considered
his most becoming attitude. Just as he was irrascably* (sic) *seated, some 'lady friends'*

---

[i] In France, the rank equivalent to the English earl.

of his appeared on the walk about, and on seeing him called out 'Ach wie schön!'

(Ah, how beautiful) which must have been trying - however, the portrait was a success.

Emily Mary's travel diary hints at the continuing fragilility of Craven's health during their tour:

5th Sept 61

Drew for three hours - the result not so great as might have been expected - studied German declensions till I felt the hopelessness of ever learning that language to perfection - William was invited to go out shooting again, but declined the sport as it was to be the same as the former occasion and only to begin in the damp hours of evening.

And at the end of October:

William's eye was rather inflamed, so he did not go out.

By this time, they had proceeded by way of Switzerland to Italy, and were in Genoa, about to embark on a sea voyage down the coast: Livorno, Elba, and Sicily, where Emily Mary reports making a sketch of Mount Pellegrino, near Palermo, while Evelyn *took a very successful view*. Returning north via Naples, where Craven's grandmother spent her final years,[i] the party arrived in Rome in time to celebrate Christmas. Curiously unperturbed by the threat of violence in an Italy then in the throes of revolution,

---

[i] Elizabeth, Margravine of Anspach, left her Naples home, Palazzino Chiatamone, and her other properties, to her youngest son, Keppel Richard Craven, uncle of the photographer. Keppel died in 1851 and his son Augustus, inherited. (In the family tree of the descendents of the Margravine, Broadley and Melville show Keppel as having died unmarried and without issue. Though he was indeed unmarried, he had a son, Augustus, by an unnamed woman and he brought the boy up as his own son and heir - see M.C. Bishop: *Mrs. Augustus Craven (Pauline de la Ferronnays)*, London, 1894, vol. I, pp.32 & 72. Augustus lived in the Palazzino Chiatamone from 1853, though he also took a house in Berkeley Square. The V&A Museum has an album of photographs by various authors (ref:X625) which contains a portrait titled in ink: *L. Wingfield, Mr. A. Craven (photo) Naples/58.* The album also contains carte-de-visite size portraits of Augustus Craven and his wife, Pauline de la Ferrona.

and—strangely—omitting any mention of the death of Albert, Prince Consort, which occurred on 14th December, Mary's diary for the year ends with a grim reflection on the chances of Britain being drawn into the American Civil War, which had by then been raging for some months. The satirical magazine, *Punch*, quipped:

> *Though with the North we sympathise*
> *It must not be forgotten*
> *That with the South we've stronger ties*
> *Which are composed of cotton*

In the event, war with America was averted. The Cravens travelled on to Paris, and thence home in the spring of 1862. Mary's photographic pursuit of Franz turned out to be nothing more than a passing fancy, and shortly after returning to England she married George John Brudenell-Bruce, son of the Marquess of Ailesbury.

Craven's major preoccupation was now Combe Abbey. The rebuild was William Eden Nesfield's first grand commission, with one wing to be demolished and replaced by a major new structure in the neo-Gothic style, the remainder of the existing fabric to be refurbished, staff quarters extended and new stabling provided—for all of which he acknowledged his gratitude to his patron with the dedication of his book, *Specimens of Mediæval Architecture*, published in 1862. At the same time, William Andrews Nesfield's redesign of the garden was implemented. The work at Combe—and the expense—would burden Craven's remaining days. Even then, it remained unfinished at his death. Almost four years after work commenced, in January 1866, Emily Mary would write to Kate:

> *We have had wretched weather since we came here and poor old Craven wishes himself*
> *back in Charles Street most part of the twenty four hours. The place is in too great a*
> *mess, but I do think what is being done will be a great success some of these days.*

Although she would recover and live to be eighty-six, surviving Queen Victoria's death in January 1901 by four months, Emily Mary too was suffering ill-health at this period. She complained of arthritic pains, and in her letters to Kate she excuses the uncontrolled scrawl of her handwriting, which was caused by deteriorating eyesight. On occasion, she was obliged to dictate her letters to one of her daughters or to a companion. In April 1863, their mother, Lady Grimston, died. Kate lamented:

> *That kind loving spirit is gone to its rest.*

201

Two weeks later Kate records:

> *Emily Craven came for a few hours from Eton where she is staying to nurse*
> *her boy Osbert who has been dangerously ill indeed is not yet out of danger.*[111]

Osbert would recover from his undefined illness, but Fate now decided that the Cravens had thusfar escaped too lightly, and from then on death crowded in on the family. The previously recounted manner of Frederick Craven's death the following year—of alcohol-related diseases—was inevitable, only the timing could not be predicted; but nothing could have prepared Craven and his wife for what was to follow. The causes of the tragedy are unexplained. Prior letters from Emily Mary no longer exist, and Kate's diaries ring no alarm bells. On 18th April 1865, when Emily Mary's chief preoccupation should have been with the imminent wedding of Beatrix Jane—Beattie—instead, on the black-edged notepaper of mourning, she writes pitiably of a loss as grievous as any that parents can suffer—the death of their eldest son and heir:

> *My Darling Kate,*
>
> *It was not from not <u>feeling</u> all your kindness and sympathy that I have not yet written,*
> *but all exertion has been painful to me, and I knew you would not misconstrue my*
> *silence. Thank Heaven Craven has got over the trial effectively without suffering*
> *in health, but oh! it has been a terrible trial and one has need to turn absolutely*
> *to all the blessings one has left, to prevent one's declining. It came so quickly at*
> *last. The day I wrote to you I certainly felt he was in great danger, but that I should*
> *lose him before another day had dawned never entered my head I sat with him. that*
> *evening till 11 o'clock and I fancied the last hour or two he was sleeping quietly and*
> *not half an hour afterwards Chelsea called us in by the nurse's report as she said*
> *he was sinking fast, and he never spoke or moved again, going off so gently without*
> *a shadow of a struggle that we could hardly tell when it was all over. I never am*
> *a good hand at talking of religion and finding out what people think, but if as*
> *pure a life as ever a human being had, & patience under many and great*
> *sufferings can render anyone fit for Heaven I feel sure my poor boy is now among*
> *the blessed and that Christ who died for sinners will have purged him from any*
> *taint remaining......*

Chelsea is gone today to London having so kindly given up being with his family at
Easter & helping us thro' all our miseries; but my poor Beattie is getting to look
more and more worn, that I think we have determined the marriage shall not
be put off, at least only the few days necessary now to get things arranged....
I don't know whether the world will call this indecent, if it does I can't help it;
the marriage now could not be a gay one even if put off.... I don't see that any
more delay can do any good and may do much harm.

Even in the depths of her pain and despair, Emily Mary retained her practical and forthright manner. Beattie was married to Viscount Chelsea little more than a month after the death of her brother. The tally of disaster, however, was not yet complete.

At the age of thirteen, Robert Walter—Bob—the cheeky hand-on-hip infant in the first group photograph of the Craven children, joined the Royal Navy training ship, HMS *Britannia*, intent on a career in the navy. Two years later (and by bizarre coincidence, just before another sister's wedding— Blanche was due to marry the Earl of Coventry) Bob was thrown from his horse when it panicked on approaching the gate leading into the stableyard. Emily Mary writes to Kate:[i]

...The creature sprang at the gate, which he could not quite accomplish,
so fell over and of course Bob fell himself on his right side and broke his
left collar bone, which they say is always the case - to me that sounds odd.
....Dear old Bob is going on as well as possible and remains in good spirits, but
I am afraid he will not be able to ride again for a couple of months. It is a mercy
he was not killed.... Bob hopes to be able to get about walking soon and manage
somehow to drive to go to Blanche's wedding. He is going to sell his horses
at Tatersall's of course, he can't hunt.

Bob recovered and was passed out as a midshipman later that year apparently fit enough to be given his first appointment, to an ageing thousand-ton paddle frigate, HMS *Spiteful*, about to set sail for South America. Alas, his first voyage would also be his last. He died on board ship, off Montevideo, on 5th March 1866. The cause of his death is unrecorded.

---

[i] There is no mention in this letter, dated 14th January 1865, of Uffie being ill. Since Uffie died in mid-April, and in her letter to Kate after Uffie's death Emily Mary refers to 'the day I wrote to you', it is clear that there is much missing correspondence here, as there is elsewhere.

Even in an age of untreatable illnesses and sudden death, when without warning parents lost their children and children their siblings, to be so cruelly deprived in such a short span of time of his mother, his brother, and his eldest and his youngest sons devastated Craven beyond bearing. In the summer of 1866, in poor health, but unaccompanied by Emily Mary, he left for Scarborough, famous for the curative powers of its mineral waters. Easy of access since the arrival of the railway in the 1840s, it was a fashionable resort, and Craven had often spent some part of his summers there in the past. On Wednesday, 22nd August, Kate recorded in her diary:

A day or two before I heard from Emily Craven that poor Craven had had an attack of paralysis at Scarborough and she went off directly to him - dreadfully frightened - she had a terrible journey but found him better. They were hopeful for a day or two but August 25th I heard from her that the case was all but hopeless.

Craven had suffered his third and final stroke. On 25th August, Kate wrote:

Poor Craven expired this day!! the most unselfish creature that ever breathed....

The Times reported:

We regret to record the death of the Earl of Craven, which took place at Scarborough on Saturday morning, the 25th inst. It has been his Lordship's practice to visit Scarborough during the season for several years past. His Lordship arrived at Scarborough this year on 1st August, and was seized with paralysis on one side - a similar attack to the one he sustained about eight years ago. The symptoms of paralysis gradually abated until Wednesday last, when Dr. Cook found the other side was seriously threatened. Thence-forward his Lordship's condition became alarming, and he gradually sank and expired, as before stated, on Saturday forenoon. Lady Craven, Lady Emily Craven, Lord and Lady Chelsea, and the Hon. Osbert Craven were present at the death of the Earl.

Wednesday 29th August, Kate:

I went to my poor broken hearted sister at Combe Abbey and stayed with her till over the funeral which took place at Combe on Saturday the 1st September 1866. Clarendon joined me at Combe on the day before, Friday 31st Aug to attend the sad ceremony next day - oh what wretched scenes of misery

In May 1836, in the second of a series of lectures on the history of landscape painting given at the Royal Institution of Great Britian (whose journal first reported Tom Wedgwood's attempts to make a photographic image in 1802) John Constable said:

> *No doubt the greatest masters considered their best efforts but as experiments,*
> *and perhaps as experiments that had failed when compared with their hopes,*
> *their wishes, and with what they saw in nature.*[112]

In the early 1860s—late in his days—now numbered—Craven reassessed his photographic works and determined that they should survive him. After the publication of William Eden Nesfield's *Specimens of Mediæval Architecture*, Craven commissioned the magnificent album that would become his memorial. The exterior of the massive album and its ornately illuminated title page are characteristic of Victorian decorative art in the neo-Gothic style—Nesfield's style. The design and the title page were almost certainly executed by Nesfield himself (he was an accomplished artist as well as an architect) with input from Craven. So fine a piece of handcrafting as the album would have been expensive, and conventionally it might be expected that the armorial furniture mounted on the album cover would have been of sterling silver. Instead, idiosyncratically, it is of base metal, electro-plated, in tune with Craven's interest in modern technologies. The album covers are of tooled morocco, mounted with decorative and armorial devices. The hinge of the album clasp is formed of the family coat-of-arms flanked by armorial supporters, *Two Griffins, wings elevated, ermine, beaked and membered, or*. Subscribed, in a scroll, is the family motto, *Virtus in Actione Consistit*—Virtue Consists in Action. Affixed centrally to the face is the letter *C*, contained within a decorative cartouche, a variant of William Craven's cypher; the device being surmounted by an earl's coronet, the whole contained within decorative cornerpieces. The title page of the album consists of an elaborate polychrome hand-illuminated leaf in which the capital *T* of *The* appears also ambiguously to be a *C* for Craven, forming the radial point of a border containing the title, *A Record of the Earl of Craven's Photographic Experiments*.

A record of The Earl of Craven's Photographic Experiments

1866

Images were assembled for the three main sections of the album: family, trees, parterre, plus a few other old favourites, a total of one-hundred-and-nine prints. Probably working with his photographer daughter, Evelyn Mary, Craven indicated how the individual leaves of the album should be laid out, some bearing single large-format prints, others combining groups of smaller images in juxtapositions that were the fulfillment of his original vision. At the point at which Craven, through ill-health, lost his grip on the project, he had given identifications to only some of the portrait subjects—those that Evelyn Mary might not herself have recognised. These were left with names lightly pencilled below them. In the finished album all would have been calligraphed in ornamental Gothic script. Evelyn Mary was not fully instructed in the proper final order of the leaves, so that the chronology has gone awry; and the waveringly uncertain edges of the scroll bearing the date *1866* on the title page of the album, inserted post mortem, were not drawn by the same steady hand that executed the main part of the finely illuminated leaf. Commenced late in the day, the album was intended by Craven as a valediction. Unfinished at his untimely death, it became his epitaph.

The title of the album, *A Record of the Earl of Craven's Photographic Experiments*, might be lightly dismissed as referring to nothing more than Craven's mastery of the ferociously demanding techniques of the wet-collodion process. It is certainly a title of Craven's own devising, for who but the man himself would have described its contents so tentatively—and, on the face of it, with such self-abjuring modesty—as *Experiments*, a word which might seem suggestive of the inner doubts of a self-taught artist who has chosen to defy the mainstream, and then avoided submitting even his best works to the judgement of his peers—for Craven participated in only two of the annual exhibitions that were the main forum for debating the art of photography in the 1850s. Yet there is a dichotomy here. Craven had the boldness to go where his imagination led him. There are signs neither of timorousness nor of hesitancy in the extant work, not in the folios nor in the album, even when, as inevitably happens on occasion, the results do not live up to the aspiration—for not every surviving image can claim to be a masterpiece. By this account, the term *Experiments* takes on a much more robust meaning. It is assertive, self-confident. The experiments are successful and worthy of being part of the record. They are not just a demonstration of mastery over the techniques of the photographic process. They are descriptive of an intense period of creative exploration, insight and exegesis which opened up new worlds. The creative, right side of the equation finally asserts its dominance over the left, the latter dictating the conventions that had long governed the English gentry, who still looked with a distaste approaching horror on the idea of taking any bar country pursuits too seriously.

Craven's final self-portrait—standing beside his great camera, still elegant in his satin-trimmed suit of velvet, a little hunched, aged beyond his years, his semi-paralysed left arm supported on the camera platform—has only one possible interpretation: that while his station in life was his birthright, his dedication to photography was of his choosing. This is as close as Craven would ever come to a public declaration of his hidden desire to be remembered for his art. After a century-and-a-half the wish has been granted. Craven has taken his rightful place in the pantheon of the great photographer-artists of his time.

Appendix:
Gustave Le Gray and The Arrival of the Body of Admiral Bruat

Given the continuing high level of interest shown in the wondrous and varied seascapes of Gustave Le Gray and, as indicated earlier, the lack of documentation relating to their creation, it is not surprising to find certain differences of opinion arising as to the precise subject matter of some of them, where and how they were achieved, and their chronology. One of the most intense and romantic of the images depicts a flotilla of French vessels, the last generation of these great wooden-hulled warships, moored off an unidentified coastline, under a sky filled with drifting cumulus clouds. Some of the ships are discharging their cannon, leaving a haze of whitish smoke hanging in the air. A print of this treasured image was amongst the nine Le Gray seascapes in the Craven collection. It was untitled.

In *The Photography of Gustave Le Gray* [113] another copy of the photograph is referred to by the author, Eugenia Parry Janis (who named it as one of three previously unpublished Le Gray seascapes she had located) as *The Arrival of the Body of Admiral Bruat and the Flagship 'Montebello' at Toulon, Dec 2-3 1855*, this title having been found inscribed on the mount. Janis credits the print to the San Francisco dealer in photographic images, Robert Koch, however neither Janis nor Koch profess any knowledge of how the print came to be so inscribed. Unfortunately, the print itself was lost in a fire a number of years ago,[114] ruling out any further examination. Koch subsequently acquired a further print of the image, which bears no inscription. Yet another print of the same image had been reproduced earlier in the auction catalogue of Christie's South Kensington (evidently unbeknown to Janis) as lot 248 in their sale of 15th March 1979. This print was catalogued as *The Arrival of the Body of Admiral Bruat at Toulon, 3rd December 1855,* and it will be accounted for in the narrative that follows. Finally, of possibly no more than five documented copies, there is a print in the extensive Le Gray collection of the Museum of Fine Arts, Troyes, which is untitled, being identified only by its catalogue number: D46.19.594. This print was exhibited in the major retrospective of Le Gray's work at the Bibliothèque nationale de France in 2002, and published in the accompanying catalogue (pl. 174/cat. no. 157) under the title *Salves de la flotte française à Cherbourg/Salvos of the French Fleet, Cherbourg, August 1858*. A year earlier Ken Jacobson, a well-known dealer in photographic images and a reputable scholar of nineteenth century photography, had published a monograph entitled *The Lovely Sea View: A Study of the Marine Photographs published by Gustave Le Gray, 1856–1858*, in which he identified the image under discussion as *Plate 14, French/British naval fleets at Cherbourg showing gun salute, 4-8 August 1858*. Thus, to summarize, we have:

Craven's copy	untitled
Christie's	catalogued as *Admiral Bruat*
Koch (1)	(destroyed in a fire) inscribed *Admiral Bruat*
Koch (2)	untitled
Museum of Troyes	untitled. Catalogue number only.
Jacobson	*Cherbourg* (his reproduction is of the Craven copy)
Bibliothèque nat.	*Cherbourg* (after Jacobson? Reproduction of the Troyes copy)

Jacobson observes that: *It is now possible to present considerable evidence, however, that the English inscription on the print discovered by Janis relating to Admiral Bruat must be an error. The supposed 1855 'Bruat' series described by Janis was actually a group of photographs produced at some festivities in Cherbourg in the summer of 1858. The most convincing proof of this comes from another extant print from Janis' supposed 1855 series (seen in our figure 11).*[115] *Our figure 11 is copied from a print in the Royal Archives which comes from Queen Victoria's personal collection. The inscription on the original mount of the Royal Archive print reads, 'French Fleet at Cherbourg Aug 5th 1858'. According to the consensus amongst archivists at the Royal Archives, the writing is in the hand of Prince Albert himself.*

Whoever may have been the author of this inscription—and there is no reason to suppose that it was not Prince Albert—there is no more evidence that it is correct than that the *Admiral Bruat* inscription on the Koch print was incorrect. In fact, as Jacobson himself points out,[116] the copy of this image in the Craven collection bore a contemporary inscription identifying it (in *French!*) as being of the French fleet at Brest, but Brest is then crossed out and Cherbourg subsituted, which would seem to indicate that a degree of confusion reigned all round when it came to labelling the prints at the point of origin. We can therefore draw no conclusions.

Jacobson's account continues:

The strip of land in the distance of figure 11 appears to be the same as that in the other two prints Janis thinks are from 1855. Thus, all three of Janis' supposed 1855 prints and in fact, most of the Le Gray views showing fleets of ships, were actually taken in 1858 at Cherbourg. Moreover, the dramatically captured gun salute.... allegedly signalling arrival of the body of Admiral Bruat, is most likely a welcoming salute for Queen Victoria and Prince Albert, who arived at Cherbourg on 4th August 1858.

The identification of the *strip of land* (that is, the only truly identifiable part of it, the rising ground on the right) will be dealt with in due course, but whilst there can be no doubt that Jacobson's researches in general have added vastly to the meagre store of knowledge concerning Le Gray's seascapes, and locating them at Cherbourg carries conviction in the case of *some* of them, one might be forgiven for harbouring considerable doubts about his contention that *most of the Le Gray views showing fleets of ships* belonged to the events that took place there in 1858.

For myself, seeing the Craven copy of *Admiral Bruat* (as I shall continue to call it for the sake of convenience, until proven) emerge from the folio was like meeting an old friend after a long separation, for I had been familiar with this rare image since the late 1970s, having included it in one of the films I was directing for Granada Television in their series on the history of nineteenth century photography. The film episode in question was about the developing portrayal of newsworthy events in photographs. Commencing in the 1840s these were included, where available, in the form of woodblock engravings taken from them, in the new weekly news magazines, such as the *Illustrated London News* in England and *L'Illustration* in France. Original photographic images of newsworthy events of the nineteenth century are extraordinarily rare, and this—the dramatic *Admiral Bruat* image—though never reproduced, could only have been taken for a very special reason, such as a direct commission; indeed, an imperial command.

Throughout a period lasting from the 1852 portrait, at which time as the Prince-President Louis-Napoleon Bonaparte he was emperor-in-waiting, to the photographs of the army excercises at Châlons in 1857, Le Gray enjoyed Napoleon III's patronage. If bidden to attend the arrival the *Montebello* bearing the body of another of the Emperor's favourites, Le Gray could hardly have refused, despite being engaged at the time with the installation of his new studio in the boulevard des Capucines. In his time, Admiral Bruat ranked second only to Admiral Courbet as a French naval commander. He took part in every major French naval action from the 1820s on and was appointed governor of Tahiti and subsequently governor-general of the Antilles before being posted to the Crimea in 1855. He was then still a vice-admiral. In the absence of the British fleet Bruat distinguished himself by successfully achieving the evacuation of the allied forces from the beseiged town of Sebastopol, as a reward for which he was raised to full admiral by Napoleon III. Bruat died suddenly of typhus, to which he fell victim on board his flagship the *Montebello* as it rounded Cape Matapan (Akra Tainaron) at the southernmost tip of the Greek coast, on 19th November 1855, while en route for his home port. The *Montebello* docked at Toulon, headquarters of the French Mediterranean fleet, on 2nd December, and the Admiral's body was brought ashore for obsequies on the 3rd. His mortal remains were then transferred to Paris (via Marseille, as we shall see) where a forewarned government had arranged a state funeral. Bruat was interred at the Père Lachaise cemetery, leaving his Emperor to mourn his lost officer.

Sentiment, however, was of less importance than providing for a state funeral as a piece of political theatre. In the aftermath of the Crimean War Napoleon III became intent on asserting his authority as the senior partner in Anglo-French entente, and the significance of this show of solidarity with his navy, underscoring Bruat's achievement at Sebastopol, and by implication that of the navy, would not be lost on its audience. Two-and-a-half years on it would be Queen Victoria's chagrin at the display of France's naval superiority over the British that would cause to her to quit Cherbourg before the completion of the planned ceremonies there, in August 1858.

Occasionally, amongst the thousands of images under review while making the Granada Television film series in the 1970s, one of uncertain title would emerge that required deeper research in order to verify it. At the time, I suspected that *Admiral Bruat* would turn out to be such a case, for I was aware that there were few records left by Le Gray. Yet the image was brought to me by my researcher complete with title and description of the event. I knew the researcher to be conscientious in the extreme, and the production team to whom she was responsible to be absolutely scrupulous in checking titles and attributions. Since no one at the time voiced any doubts there was no reason for me to single out this, amongst the masses of photographs I was dealing with, for further checks. Thus, it came as something of a surprise to read of Jacobson's reattribution of the image. Could he possibly be right? Could this really be one of the Cherbourg images? I was determined to see what might be done to solve the mystery.

The Montebello flying its flag at half-mast.

Before giving an account of the results of my own researches, some observations are called for with regard to Jacobson's account. Aside from the unlikelihood of attaching quite such an arcane label—by implication accidentally—as *The Arrival of the Body of Admiral Bruat* to such a recognisable celebration as that which took place nearly three years later at Cherbourg, the first matter that draws one's attention is the reproduction of the wood engraving from the *Illustrated London News* of 14th August 1858, entitled, *The Cherbourg Fetes—Arrival of Her Majesty at Cherbourg*, which Jacobson calls as witness.[117] The arrangement of the vessels in the picture is striking. In the foreground, to the left of centre, we see the steam-powered royal yacht, the *Victoria and Albert* (launched in 1843). At the mastheads it will be flying the royal standard, the Union Jack, and the flag of the escorting squadron (the organisation of British naval forces into squadrons was not terminated until 1864) and at the stern, the red ensign. The right-hand side of the engraving is dominated by eight or more warships, forming an unwavering line into the distance. They are firing a gun salute. There is no image in any of Le Gray's published work that remotely resembles this festive scene, in particular as to the formal stationing of the warships. If confirmation were needed that this was not an artist's fanciful interpretation of the vista, it is to be found in a contemporary coloured lithograph by the French marine artist, Louis Lebreton, which depicts the exact same scene from a different

216

angle. Apart from the variation of viewpoint, these two images correspond in their main essentials, excepting that Lebreton has ommitted to show the sailors lining the spars, a traditional part of such royal occasions. It is very likely that Lebreton acquired a sketch of the scene from another artist[i] who had not included the sailors lining the spars, and that he worked it up into the lithograph for publication. Lebreton's lithograph is titled, *Arrivée de la Reine Victoria à Cherbourg et vaisseaux de ligne*. It is one piece out of a series entitled, *Voyage de S.M. l'empereur dans l'ouest*. In contrast to the formal array of ships-of-the-line seen in these two prints, the vessels in the *Admiral Bruat* photograph are moored in a casual group. There is no point of correspondence between the graphic prints and the *Admiral Bruat* photograph beyond the fact that they both show a gun salute.

The flags that bedeck the warships raise the second and yet more significant point at issue. The pennants at the main topmasts are clearly visible in the *ILN* engraving. They are quartered, with the Union Jack at the top inner corner. The darker ground of the remaining quarters of the pennants indicates that they are the red ensign of the British Navy (Admiralty orders replacing the red with the white as the senior naval ensign did not come into force until 1864. Thereafter, the red ensign was used only by the merchant fleet). This again is confirmed by the coloured lithograph of Lebreton, in which the red ground is quite clearly observable.

Arrivée de la Reine Victoria à Cherbourg
et vaisseaux de ligne. Coloured lithograph
by Louis Lebreton, 1858.

---

[i] For a comparison, see below: the account of Dr Jacquot.

217

In order to learn something of the protocols governing the use of naval flags, I consulted Commander Bruce Nicolls, OBE, RN (Rtd) an acknowledged expert in the subject. First, I was informed, one could read nothing meaningful from the extensive display of signal flags seen at Cherbourg, which would have been there for decorative purposes only. On a ceremonial occasion such as this they would, for obvious reasons, have been hung deliberately to avoid showing any signal that the ships might have used while at sea. Second, protocol on a state visit would have dictated that the visitors' flags be flown in the dominant position at the main topmast, with the hosts' pennant below, and/or at the fore and mizzen masts. This is the arrangement as pictured in the *ILN* illustration as well as in the Lebreton lithograph, that is, with the Union flags above the French, and it would have applied for the occasion on all the ships-of-the-line, French or British.

The Montebello flying its flag at half-mast

Now, there is no British naval flag in evidence anywhere in *any* of Le Gray's photographs of ships. All of the ships in Jacobson's *pl.14* (identified by Janis and by myself as *Admiral Bruat*) and his *pl.15* (which he identifies as being taken at Cherbourg) are flying the French tricolore at all three mastheads. It would appear possible, then, that Le Gray executed a number of photographs of the French fleet in preparation for the arrival of Queen Victoria (e.g. Jacobson *pl.15*) but before the French had run up the British colours in honour of their guests, or after the queen had left, when they had struck the colours. Strangely, there is no known Le Gray image of the welcoming ceremony itself. While any explanation proposed is necessarily speculative, it is at least worth considering the possibility that, if he was indeed present, Le Gray was unable to find a camera position close enough to the ceremony to have produced the kind of dramatic scene which the engraving and the lithograph depict. Neither did any other photographer. So much for photographic realism.

The flag as flown normally. Detail of a lithograph by Louis Lebreton.

Commander Nicolls made two further observations relating to the flags displayed in the *Admiral Bruat* image. First, the ships are showing only what is described as 'lesser flags', that is, they are not celebratory, unlike the engraving and the lithograph referred to, which show the ships in full fig. Secondly, and crucially, the three decker to the left of centre of the *Admiral Bruat* photograph *is flying its tricolore at half-mast*. It is categorically impossible that a ship flying its main flag at half-mast should have been taking part in a celebration, since at the time a flag flown at half-mast signified mourning, as it still does today.

218

At this point it seemed to me high time to try and seek to retrace the origins of the copy of *Admiral Bruat* that I had used in my film, and to see if anything further might emerge. Miraculously, considering that a quarter of a century had passed by, I was able to locate the person who then owned the photograph, having found his name, George Grima, amongst the picture credits in the book that accompanied the film series.[118] Mr Grima told me that he had purchased the dust-covered photograph for the gilt frame that contained it, from a junk shop in north-west London early in 1978, for the princely sum of two pounds. The photograph was untitled. Though he had no knowledge of nineteenth century photography Mr Grima was perceptive enough to realise, once he had cleaned the picture glass of its coating of grime, that he had found something of quality, and he was sufficiently curious about it to try and identify it. His first port of call, if one may be permitted the pun, was the National Maritime Museum at Greenwich, whose expert could be forgiven for not being able to identify the precise occasion of the photograph, which had, after all, nothing to do with British naval history. But, having noted the prevalence of the tricolore, the expert did comment that, *It has to be very much a French affair because of the lack of the flag from any other country.* [119] The letter continues, *I am a little puzzled as to why the three decker in the centre of the picture has her flag at half mast*—the second such expert's reference.

Nothing daunted, the tenacious Mr Grima next contacted the Musée de la Marine in Paris. On 12th September 1978 he received their reply, from which I quote:

Nous avons reussi... à identifier la scène réprésentée par la photographie.... Il s'agit du retour à Toulon du corps de l'amiral Bruat, le 3 décembre 1855.... Il rentrait en France à bord de son vaisseau-amiral, le trois ponts Montebello et cinq autres vaisseaux mixtes, lorsqu'il fut pris... d'une infection aigue, le cholera sans doute, qui devait l'emporter le 19 novembre... Le Montebello et les navires qui l'accompagnaient arrivèrent le 2 décembre et le corps de l'amiral Bruat fut débarqué le 3... On reconnait au centre de la photo le Montebello (avec son pavilion en berne à corne d'artimon). Les autres bâtiments portent le petit pavois. Un salut à coups de canon est exécuté.

In translation:

We have succeeded in identifying the scene represented by the photograph. It shows the return to Toulon of the body of Admiral Bruat, on the 3rd December 1855. He was returning to France on board his flagship, the three-deck Montebello, together with five other various vessels, when he was seized by a fever, cholera no doubt, which carried him off on 19th November. The Montebello and the accompanying vessels arrived on 2nd December and the body of Admiral Bruat was disembarked on 3rd. The Montebello is recognisable at the centre of the photo (with its flag at half-mast at the peak of the mizzen gaff). The other ships are flying their lesser flags. The cannon are firing a salute.[120]

This was the third unprompted expert reference to the flag flying at half-mast, as well as the wealth of other confirmatory details.

Mr Grima offered his great discovery for sale at Christie's in London on 15th March 1979. It was catalogued as *lot 248*, as noted above, complete with the identification provided by the Musée de la Marine and their colleagues at the Service Historique. It remained unsold. Offered subsequently at Sotheby's on 24th October 1979 as *lot 87* the photograph achieved the then significant sum of £2,200. So far as I have been able to discover, no copy of the image so authoritatively identified had been sold prior to this,[121] nor have I been able, to date, to find it illustrated and described in any earlier work on nineteenth century photography, so to Mr Grima go the laurels.

The events surrounding the death of Admiral Bruat, as they unfolded, would have given Le Gray ample time to be briefed, travel to Toulon, and set up for the photograph.

The French fleet passing through the waters of the Bosphorus.
From a wood engraving by Lebreton, after a sketch by Dr Jacquot.

On 12th November 1855, the French fleet entered the waters of the Bosphorus, making a leisurely passage from Black Sea to the Mediterranean en route to their home port. As they sailed majestically past the royal palace at Scheragan, with the steam yacht of the French ambassador to Turkey at their head, the warships fired a twenty-one gun salute in honour of the Turkish sultan, an ally of the British and French in the

Crimean War. Close by, the sailors of the British fleet lying at anchor raised a mighty cheer as the matelots passed. A vivid description of the scene was contained in a letter addressed to the editor of *L'Illustration* by Dr Jacquot, surgeon-in-chief of the hospital at Pera, Constantinople. Dr Jacqot also made a lightning sketch of the scene, which he forwarded to the marine artist Louis Lebreton for completion, confident that he would give it life and render it with the necessary accuracy of detail. There was, at that moment, no shadow of warning of the tragedy to follow.

On 20th November 1855. The ship's journal of the *Montebello* [i] records the sending of the following dispatch to the Head of the Mediterranean Squadrons, Toulon. The entry is unsigned, but was presumably made by the *Montebello's* first officer, Lt de Freycinet.

J'ai la douleur de vous annoncer l'affreux malheur qui vient de nous frapper. M. l'Amiral Bruat a succombé hier à trois heures de l'après midi à une attaque de cholerà. J'envoi son neveu M. Émîle Bruat Lieut. porter cette cruelle nouvelle à Mme. l'Amiral Bruat. Je lui dira que l'Amiral est mort en Chrétien qu'il a reçu avec fervour et lorsqu'il avait encore toute sa connaissance, le dernier sacrement.

It is with grief that I inform you of the dreadful misfortune that has struck us. Yesterday, at three o'clock in the afternoon, Admiral Bruat succumbed to an attack of cholera. I am dispatching his nephew, Lt. Emile Bruat, to carry this cruel news to Madame Bruat. I will tell her that the admiral died in Christ, and that he received the last sacrement with fervour and while still in full possession of his senses.

The news was telegraphed to the Minister of the Navy, in Paris, by Rear-Admiral Jurien, head of administration at Toulon, followed by a query as to whether the body should be brought to Toulon, the home port of the Mediterranean fleet, or directed to Marseille, recently connected by rail to Paris. The Minister telegraphed his reply on 28th November. For the honour of the Navy, it was to be Toulon....

Le corps sera débarqué, et une cérémonie funèbre et religieuse sera célébrée à terre aux frais de la Marine.... Mon premier Aide de camp partira demain pour Toulon où il me représentera....

The body should be disembarked and religious funerary rites performed ashore, at the expense of the navy.... My chief aide-de-camp will depart tomorrow for Toulon, where he will represent me.

---

[i] Effectively, the ship's private diary, not to be confused with the log book, which provides a daily record of the ship's voyage, as to weather, manoeuvres, and incidents.

The period that elapsed between the news of Bruat's death reaching Paris and the arrival of the body, would have allowed Le Gray adequate time to travel down to Toulon and liaise with the office of the maritime authorities about where the *Montebello* and the other vessels comprising the flotilla—the *Fleurus, Friedland, Jean Bart, Alger* and *Primaguet*—would be moored, enabling him to locate a suitable camera position. In the event, the mooring would be offshore beyond the confines and to the east of the inner harbour of Toulon, presumably to avoid any possible risk of infection being carried to the city. The log book of *Montebello* shows her reaching her anchorage at Toulon—but not in the *rade* (i.e. harbour) itself, at nine o'clock on the morning of 2nd December. The weather was fine at first, turning overcast with occasional bright intervals, and calm, which it remained through the rest of the day and the day following. From midday on 2nd a cannon salute would be fired at regular intervals until the completion of the ceremonies and the re-embarkation of mortal remains of Admiral Bruat for Paris. It would be pointless to attempt to ascribe any specific motive to the Emperor in thus dispatching Le Gray to record the arrival of the deceased hero; men of power gesture, and we rush to obey. Sufficient to point out that, like Queen Victoria and Prince Albert, Napoleon III was quick to realize the potential of the photograph on paper, the infinitely replicable image, as a new channel of communication, a vehicle for propaganda. It was Le Gray's 1852 portrait, sold widely in print shops throughout France, that popularised the image of Napoleon III, and it would be another image of the Emperor that would launch the craze for the carte-de-visite at the end of the decade. Equally, Prince Albert was the instigator of Roger Fenton's coverage of the war in the Crimea; and in 1857 the Emperor would commission Le Gray to photograph the French army manoeuvres at Châlons. What might be photographed, was. From this moment on, whether or not published as an engraving in the journals, the photographic image would provide an increasingly vigorous challenge to the primacy of the written word.

Bruat's family, who had arrived from Paris, attended a requiem mass in the cathedral. Funerary rites were performed with due pomp and ceremony at the arsenal, dignified by a eulogy delivered by Vice-Admiral, the Baron du Bourdieu, Maritime Prefect for Toulon, who the following day wrote an account of the proceedings to the Minister of the Navy:

Le corps de l'amiral a été reçu sous un cénotaphe décoré avec le meilleur goût, et orné à ses quatres angles de faisceaux de drapeaux nationaux, de canons et d'armes Russes....

The body of the admiral was received on a cenotaph decorated in the best of taste, and ornamented at all four corners with stacked national flags, cannons and Russian arms.

'The body should be disembarked and religious funerary rites performed ashore'.
Wood engraving from L'Illustration, *22nd December 1855.*

Amid scenes of high emotion, Admiral Bruat was taken on board ship one last time, en route to his final resting place. Rear-Admiral Jurien to the Minister:

J'accompagnerai jusqu'à Paris les restes mortels de M. l'Amiral Bruat. Sa famille militaire a solicité la faveur de partager avec moi cette preuse mission.... M. l'Amiral Bruat sera donc entouré, jusqu'au dernier moment, des officiers qu'il honorait de son affection et de sa confiance. Demain, lorsque ses obsèques seront terminées, ses dépuiles mortelles seront transportées à bord du Primaguet....

I will accompany the mortal remains of Admiral Bruat to Paris. His military family have beseeched of me the favour of departing with me on this gallant mission.... Thus will Admiral Bruat be surrounded, until the very last moment, with the officers whom he honoured with his affection and his trust. Tomorrow, when the obsequies are terminated, the mortal remains will be shipped on board the Primaguet....

The log book of the *Montebello* confirms the departure the following day during the morning watch of the *Primaguet*, escorted by the *Magellan* and the *Albatross*, destination Marseilles. The leave taking was again accompanied by a cannon salute.

Thanks to the unstinting aid provided by the various departments containing elements of the French naval archives, to the fact of the flag flying at half-mast, and the surrounding circumstances recounted above, it has been possible to assemble the account given here, and to dispose of the idea that the photograph in question was taken at the Cherbourg celebrations of 1858; and furthermore, to show that it was possible for Le Gray to have been present at Toulon on 2nd and 3rd December 1855, and to have taken the photograph that bears his signature. But, lacking any empirical evidence to support the case (barring, of course, the internal evidence provided by the flag flown at half-mast) the one further possibility that remained was to locate the camera position from which the photograph was taken.

In the autumn of 2003 I contacted an old friend and colleague, Christian Petron, a highly experienced diver and a superb underwater cameraman. Petron runs a marine exploration and undersea filming company based in Toulon, and is resident in Le Pradet, a suburb of Toulon. I asked Petron's help in finding the viewpoint of the photograph, suggesting—based on what seemed to be a thoroughly reasonable proposition: that the sun would be lighting the scene approximately from the South—that the photograph might have been taken looking eastwards across the Toulon searoads.[i] No, Petron, replied. The view was taken in almost precisely the opposite direction, in fact from the shoreline not more than a couple of kilometres from his home at Le Pradet.

Succumbing to the somewhat sentimental idea of taking the same scene that Le Gray had photographed on the anniversary of the original—2nd or 3rd December—I arrived in Toulon on 1st December, amidst a heavy rainstorm. The following morning the rain continued torrential. At that moment I did not know that Toulon was on the periphery of a disaster area centred on the Rhone valley to the West, where in two days six people died in heavy flooding and fifteen thousand or more were left homeless in a sea of mud.

---

[i] Which is what I had proposed—erroneously, as it turned out—in the essay in the catalogue of the Bearne's sale of 2000.

224

As luck would have it, Petron could not meet me, having been called away to Paris on business; but I was able to find a taxi willing to take me to the coast near Le Pradet. We made our way down the now treacherous coast road, which was at first disappointingly flat—Le Gray had clearly taken his photograph from an elevation. Then, just beyond a small anchorage called Les Oursinières, we discovered rising ground and then a small headland topped by a group of ruined buildings. The area was surrounded by barbed-wire and signs reading *Danger* and *Entrée Interdite*. Unwilling to be turned back at the last moment, I climbed through a gap in the wire and ascended the steep path. From the top of the headland I was able to look back across the bay towards Toulon and see the view that Le Gray saw. The promontory on the extreme right of the picture, topped by one of the fortresses guarding the approaches to Toulon, which can just about be made out in my rain-fuzzed photograph as in Le Gray's, and the lesser headland beyond, were unmistakeable. In my mind's eye, the *Montebello* was still riding at anchor halfway across the bay, with the body of Admiral Bruat aboard, waiting to be taken ashore.

The downpour, if anything, was getting worse. I could see my driver signalling frantically while I made a couple of quick exposures, hoping for the best. The point was made: if Le Gray did not take his photograph of the *The Arrival of the Body of Admiral Bruat* from this exact spot it was certainly not taken from far away. (Le Gray's photograph appears to have been taken on a lens of slightly different focal length relative to format to my own. He is also higher above sea level, but this could be because he took his photograph from the top of buildings or fortifications that no longer stand on this site).

Le Gray: detail of 'Admiral Bruat' showing the right edge of the image at the horizon.   *Author's photograph, taken from Les Oursinières looking towards Toulon.*

Just as I was considering trying to slither back down through the mud to the road, a weak sun broke through the clouds for a moment, sending a pale gleam of light across the surface of the sea from my left, as it appears in Le Gray's photograph. I paused briefly to take another shot, and suddenly remembered the weather noted in the logbook of the *Montebello* for that day: it was mainly overcast. Le Gray's photograph shows cumulus clouds in a sunlit sky. What is more, the sun is coming from the right—that is, impossibly, it would appear to be shining from the North! Thus, the clouds in *The Arrival of the Body of Admiral Bruat* are in fact printed-in from a separate negative, taken at a different time. This is the earliest example of a Le Gray seascape using combination printing, and almost certainly the point of embarkation on his series of seascapes, one of which—*The Brig*—would be exhibited to great public acclaim a year later.

Mantled in an aura of nostalgia for the days of wooden hulls and sail, *The Arrival of the Body of Admiral Bruat* is a repository of mysteries finally less resolvable than that of its identity.

To date, all illustrations of the *Admiral Bruat* image in which it is seen in the context of other Le Gray seascapes [i] show it on the page as of a size equal to its brethren, which tends to obscure the fact that it is not. Uniquely amongst over forty known sea images, *Admiral Bruat* is 22x30 cm., and from that aspect rather less impressive on the walls of a gallery than the remainder, which are prints of approximately 30x40 cm. from negatives that were probably 45x45 cm., allowing for vertical or horizontal compositions in the camera and for the trimming of borders. [ii] If we rescale *Admiral Bruat* to show it as a part of a 30x40 cm. image we discover that the dimensions of the headland on the right match those in two less dramatic exposures of the vessels at anchor. One of these, exhibited at the

---

[i] In the aforementioned works by Janis, Jacobson, the Bibliothèque nationale catalogue, and the Bearne's auction catalogue, 2000.
[ii] Of thirty illustrated in the Bibliothèque nationale catalogue one print is trimmed to panoramic format, but its longer side exceeds the larger dimension of *Admiral Bruat*.

Bibliothèque nationale and illustrated in their catalogue,[122] is taken in the mellow late afternoon light of 2nd December. The ships tally with those seen in *Admiral Bruat*. The other, from the Craven collection, is taken under an indeterminate (masked?) sky. There are additional ships present—the exposure may have been made when the maritime prefect visited the *Montebello* on the morning of 3rd December, or on the arrival of the escort ships, *Magellan* and *Albatross*. With the images shown in the same scale and the line of the horizons matched (Le Gray was nothing if not consistent) we are able to demonstrate where the original borders of the *Admiral Bruat* image lay.

'Admiral Bruat', showing the borders of the original negative by aligning the horizon with that in another image of the flotilla from the same viewpoint (both from the Craven Collection).

Now, just below the horizon of *Admiral Bruat*, at the left edge of the picture, there is an irregular dark patch which, when enlarged, reveals itself as an area of damaged negative. Partly obscured, the stern of another ship is just visible, and the whole patch shows signs of rather crude retouching. Since all the recorded prints of *Admiral Bruat* contain the same aberration, we may reasonably conclude that Le Gray never achieved an earlier print of the entire undamaged negative that he found to be totally satisfactory or he would surely have made a copy negative from it. Either the original negative of *Admiral Bruat* suffered an accident or it was deliberately mutilated during an attempt to improve on some element within it that Le Gray found unsatisfactory.

Left edge of 'Admiral Bruat'
(the Craven copy)
showing the damaged area.

Admiral Bruat' (Koch copy 2) showing part of the line scored through the negative
(visible almost the full height of this print) and the further area of damage seen towards
the bottom left of the section illustrated (digitally enhanced images from Koch copy 2).

The key to the answer appears to lie in the second Koch copy, in which the print is trimmed marginally further to the left. More of the stern of the missing vessel is visible, including part of the mizzen mast and the tricolore. Clearly visible in this print, too, is a straight, black, near-vertical line where the negative has been deliberately scored through. The damaged patch of negative occurs where some unstable fragments of emulsion have flaked off as the blade passed, and following the line down from the main area of damage we can see where a further, smaller fragment of emulsion has been chipped away.

In order to arrive at some rational explanation of the line of demarcation, so to speak, we might first look at a digital reconstruction of the image as it might originally have appeared as a 30x40 cm. image with the clouds printed in. The white line indicates the extent of all surviving copies.

Since only sea intervened between Le Gray, stationed on a spit of land, and his subject—perhaps two kilometres distant—his frame was fixed, and it would have been constituted of largely featureless sea and sky, as we have seen it (three pages earlier) in the other image of the flotilla that was found in the Craven folio; and it must not be imagined that at this early stage of his experimentation with cloudscapes[i] Le Gray would have had a very large stock of separate cloud negatives from which to select to fill an empty sky to greater effect. A possible conclusion, therefore, is that Le Gray cropped in on three sides of the image in an attempt to give it greater strength as a composition, and that the scored line is an indication to his assistants to adhere to his intended framing. The strong alternative possibility is that there were indeed further areas of unstable or otherwise damaged emulsion, and that the cropping was a matter of necessity. One alternative surely not open to Le Gray was to fail to deliver a result to his imperial master, and the two other images taken at the same location are bland by comparison with the high drama of the salvo of guns. If *The Arrival of the Body of Admiral Bruat and the Flagship Montebello* was a failure, it was a noble and glorious one.

By the end of 1856, with the death of Admiral Bruat no more than a dimly recalled event and the Crimean War beginning to fade from current memory, Le Gray had produced *The Brig*, a sea image that was more obviously dramatic to a contemporary audience than *Admiral Bruat*, for the wooden-hulled warship had not yet become a subject for nostalgic contemplation, and the presence of the billowing clouds would have held no mystery for a lay audience unaware of the continuing technical difficulties that stood in the way of capturing them. *The Brig*, however, was imbued with all the qualities of a Romantic painting, with its dark weight of cloud; its evanescent light, suggestive of moonlight; and in the distance, the lonely brig, a transient shadow bound on a mysterious mission.

---

[i] The Bibliothèque nationale catalogue shows two experimental landscapes with clouds printed-in from separate negatives (catalogue nos.73 and 74) which very probably predate *Admiral Bruat*.

Acknowledgements

My most profound thanks are due first and most obviously to Brian Bearne and Robin Barlow, both directors of Bearne's Fine Art Auctioneers of Exeter at the time of the emergence of the Craven folios. Without them I should never have met William Craven. Sadly, Brian is no longer with us, but Robin has continued to lend unstinting help and support throughout the making of this book. Next, chronologically, comes Graham Ovenden, with whom I shared the revelation of Craven's magnificent work as it emerged from the folios in which it had lain hidden for almost a century and a half. Graham has been my companion and my support throughout this journey, and his profound insights both as an artist and a photographer have been as invaluable as his patience has been endless; queries answered with wisdom and erudition, long telephone hours freely given listening to endless fragments of rewrites, and finally, when he was suffering from an eye problem, surviving an heroic session when I read him the entire work at one sitting. Much of the small amount of Craven memorabilia still extant is in the hands of Lt. Commander RJE Craven, RN (rtd) who has suffered repeated raids upon his archives with the best of grace, and who, together with his wife, Sue, has several times extended the warm hospitality of their home, as well as giving my wife and myself an introduction to the magnificence of the north coast of Scotland. Grateful thanks to David Golby, for his skills in rephotographing Craven's originals; to Daniel Goddard and Richard Bearne of Bearne's Fine Art Auctioneers, for allowing continued access to documentation; to John O'Grady for advice on photographic techniques and for the loan of a field camera on which I tried out some of my ideas on how nineteenth century photographers worked; to Russell and Susie Needham for the use of that now increasingly rare facility: an old-fashioned 'wet' darkroom in which to do my film processing; and to Penelope Stokes, author and historian of West Berkshire. The Countess of Craven and the present young Earl of Craven have kindly permitted me to quote from the correspondence and diaries of William Craven's wife, Emily Mary; Lord Clarendon from the Clarendon Papers at the Bodleian; and Mr. A.J. Maxse from the Maxse Archives, wherein I found the only manuscript note in William Craven's own hand. Lord Greenway engineered the loan of a copy of Maxwell's *Life & Letters of George Villiers, 4th Earl of Clarendon*. Harrington Rare Books kindly gave me free access to copy illustrations from Richardson's *The Eglinton Tournament*, and The Map House of Knightsbridge was equally generous in permitting me to copy a print of Roberts' *Memnonium of Thebes*. Sally Ann Mawson, of the Coombe Abbey Hotel (who have resurrected the building) drew my attention, amongst other things, to the 1909 *Country Life* article on the Abbey. Martin Barnes, Curator of Photographs at the Victoria & Albert Museum, drew my attention to the Craven family-related album in their collection. Julian Cox, Curator of Photography at the High Museum of Art, Atlanta, provided me with Gutch's words on the camera's point of view. Sir Peter Blake kindly provided the stereo of General Tom Thumb. The work in progress was read by friends, Clive Crook, Gilvrie Lock, and Stefan Stuckert; and by Michael Gray, photographic historian and ex-curator of the Fox Talbot Museum at Lacock, whose input was much valued. Without Christian Petron's advice on the topography of the Toulon area I should have been unable to locate the viewpoint from which Le Gray took *The Arrival of Admiral Bruat*, the story of which could not have been told without the efforts of the resourceful George Grima, the advice of Commander Bruce Nicolls, OBE, RN (Rtd.), and the archivists at the Musée national de la Marine, the Service Historique de la Marine, Toulon, and the Service Historique de la Marine at Vincennes. At Vincennes, Dan Salzmann, an American in Paris, helped me to decipher reems of French mid-nineteenth century copperplate. My analysis of the damage suffered by the negative of *The Arrival of Admiral Bruat* and the reasons for it, was wholly dependent on the generous provision of a scan of the scored copy of the image by Robert Koch of the Robert Koch Gallery, San Franisco. Needless to say, the opinions I have expressed in this regard, and in any other areas that may be considered to be contentious, are wholly my own, and I take full and sole responsibility for them.

My thanks, equally, to my publisher, Simon Butler, and designer, Sharon O'Inn.

Finally, I should like to note the unfailing interest, helpfulness and courtesy of every single curator, archivist and librarian whose help I have sought, especially those at the British Library, the Bodleian, the Victoria and Albert Museum, the West Sussex Record Office, the Coventry Library and Information Service, and the Centre for Buckinghamshire Studies. And since we are now well and truly into the digital age, I should like also to acknowledge the vast fund of information made available, at no gain to themselves, by the authors of a mass of websites, without whom the job would have been a great deal more difficult.

Noel Chanan

Source Notes

(Quotations retain the spellings and punctuation of the originals)

1. William C. Darrah, *Cartes de Visite in Nineteenth Century Photography*, Gettysburg, 1981, p.6.
2. Thomas Dunham Whitaker, *The History and Antiquities of the Deanery of Craven in the County of York*, 2nd edn., 1812, p.437.
3. Madden: Lady Blessington, vol. II, p.126.
4. A.M. Broadley & Lewis Melville, (eds.) *The Beautiful Lady Craven - The original memoirs of Elizabeth Baroness Craven afterwards Margravine of Anspach and Bayreuth and Princess Berkeley of the Holy Roman Empire (1750–1828). Edited and with notes and a Biographical and Historical Introduction containing much unpublished matter. London, 1914.* Vol. I (of II) p.35.
5. ibid., Vol. I, pp.32–34 & 39.
6. ibid., Vol. I, p.39.
7. ibid., Vol. II, pp.118–9.
8. ibid., Vol. I, p.38.
9. Charles Piggott, *The Jockey Club*, 3rd edn., 1792, Vol. III, p.160.
10. Broadley & Melville, Vol. I, p.53.
11. ibid., p.lxxi.
12. ibid., p.xxxiv.
13. ibid., p.11.
14. In 1942, a grandson of Evelyn Mary, the photographer's second daughter, wrote a memoir. It was published in an army magazine under the pen name Bombardier, hereafter referred to as Bombardier.
15. Broadley & Melville, Vol. I, p.50.
16. *Coventry Herald*, 3rd March 1925.
17. Bodleian, *Catalogue of the Papers of Lady Clarendon.* Ms. Eng. c 2084. Undated letter addressed to *My dearest Mamma* and signed *Mary Folkestone*.
18. Bennis, *The Paris Directory and Visitor's Guide*, Paris, 1834.
19. See the *Craven Papers* at the Bodleian Library, Oxford. Unfortunately, Lady Emily Mary Craven appears to have kept no diaries except when she was on these extended tours, or else, none has survived.
20. Letter from Lady Craven to her sister Katharine (Kate) Countess of Clarendon, undated c. 1844. Bodleian, Catalogue of the Papers of Lady Clarendon. Ms. Eng. c 2084
21. Bombardier (see ref. 14 above).
22. ibid.,
23. Warren Greene Ogden, Jr., *Notes on the History and Provenance of Holzapffel Lathes*, (privately published) North Andover, Mass., 1987.
24. Quoted in R.B. Martin, *Enter Rumour*, Faber, 1962, p.88.
25. ibid., p.120.
26. ibid., pp.111–112.
27. C.R. Leslie, *Memoirs of the Life of John Constable*, Phaidon 1995 edn., p.267.
28. ibid., extract from Constable's letter to his friend John Fisher, 1821, p.73.
29. Pichot, *Historical and Literary Tour of a Foreigner in England and Scotland*, 1825, Vol. I, quoted in Patrick Noon, *Constable to Delacroix, British Art and the French Romantics*, Tate Publishing, 2003, p.192.
30. Letter to the *Telegraph*, London, 15th August, 2000.
31. C.R. Leslie, *Memoirs of the Life of John Constable*, Phaidon 1995 edn., extract from Constable's letter to his friend John Fisher, 1821, p.234.

[32] See: Helmut & Alison Gernsheim, *LJM Daguerre - The History of the Diorama and the Daguerreotype*, 2nd revised edn., N.Y., 1968.

[33] Abbreviated from an eywitness account by Ludwig Pfau, *Kunst und Gewerbe*, Part 1, Stuttgart, 1877, quoted in Helmut & Alison Gernsheim, *L.J.M. Daguerre - The History of the Diorama and the Daguerreotype*, 2nd revised edn., 1968, pp.100–101.

[34] *Chambers Cyclopædia or An Universal Dictionary of Arts and Sciences*, 5th edn., 1743.

[35] *The English Garden*, 1772-82, vol. iv, quoted in Hussey, *The Picturesque*, 1974.

[36] *Magasin Pittoresque*, volume for 1839, p.374, (present author's translation).

[37] *Chambers's Edinburgh Journal*, No. 405, November 2nd 1839.

[38] Robison's account, first published in the *Edinburgh New Philosophical Journal*, was reported in *Chambers's Edinburgh Journal*, No. 395, August 24th 1839.

[39] Sir John Robison in *Athenaeum: Journal of English and Foreign Literature, Science, and the Fine Arts, June 8, 1839*, quoted in Maillet, *The Claude Glass*, (see below) p.177.

[40] For a complete and fascinating account of this history see: Arnaud Maillet, *The Claude Glass, Use and Meaning of the Black Mirror in Western Art*, translated by Jeff Fort, New York, 2004.

[41] Arago's report to the French Chamber of Deputies, 6th July 1839, reproduced in the original French and in translation in *Daguerre, An historical and descriptive account...* etc., edited and introduced by Beaumont Newhall, 1971.

[42] *Mirror of Literature, Amusement, and Instruction*, 19th October, 1839

[43] See Helmut & Alison Gernsheim, *LJM Daguerre - the History of the Diorama and the Daguerreotype*, London, 1956; 2nd revised edn., N.Y., 1968, pp.110–111.

[44] Quoted from Betty Miller (ed.), *Elizabeth Barrett to Miss Mitford*, London, 1954, pp.208–9

[45] Elizabeth Anne McCauley, *Industrial Madness, Commercial Photography in Paris 1848–1871.* see p.5 for wages, p.47 for cost of daguerreotypes. It is probable that in the provinces they were a good deal cheaper, though wages would also have been less. Bearne's of Exeter's sale of photographs of 12th May 2001, lot 4, details the verso of a French itinerant photographer's daguerreotypes, listing portraits from 3 Francs, still an unaffordable amount for a working man.

[46] Charles Dickens, 'Photography' in *Household Words*, no. 156, March 19th, 1853.

[47] Centre for Buckinghamshire Studies, Hawtrey Papers, D65/2/3 ('Monty' is not further identifiable).

[48] Larry J. Schaaf, *Out of the Shadows - Herschel, Talbot, & the Invention of Photography*, Yale University Press, 1992, p.85.

[49] ibid., p.85.

[50] *Photogenic Drawing, or Drawing by the Agency of Light*, In *The Edinburgh Review*, Vol. LXXVI, October 1842 - January 1843, pp.334–334. The Article in unsigned, but attributed by Gernsheim (*Incunabula* 1079) to Sir David Brewster, the journal's editor.

[51] Nadar: *Quand j'étais Photographe*, Paris, 1900, p.192. (Present author's translation).

[52] Tim Hilton, *John Ruskin*, Yale Nota Bene edn., 2002, p.480.

[53] Walter Pach (trans): *The Journal of Eugene Delacroix*, London, 1938, p.314.

[54] *Autobiography of Benjamin Robert Haydon*, The World's Classics, Oxford, 1927, p.360.

[55] Nadar: *Quand j'étais Photographe*, Paris, 1900, pp.195–7. (passage translated & edited by the present author)

[56] *Exhibition of the Works of Industry of All Nations, Reports by the Juries, in Four Volumes*, vol. II, p.520.

[57] ibid., p.522.

[58] ibid., p.607.

[59] ibid., p.597.

[60] C.R. Leslie, *Memoirs of the Life of John Constable*, Phaidon 1995 edn., p.278.

[61] Baudelaire's article is reproduced in Newhall, *Photography: Essays and Images*, reprinting it from *Charles Baudelaire, The Mirror of Art*, Phaidon Press, 1955, pp.228–31.

[62] Helmut & Alison Gernsheim, *The History of Photography from the Camera Obscura to the Beginning of the Modern Era*, 2nd edn., 1969, p.197, et seq.

[63] Gail Buckland, *First Photographs*, London, 1981, p.255.

[64] From part II of a two part article on Combe Abbey in *Country Life*, 11th December 1909.

[65] Ludwig Goldscheider (ed.) J. Byam Shaw (trans.) *Five Hundred Self-Portraits*, Phaidon, Vienna and London, 1937, nos. 15, 70, 371, respectively.

[66] Marcus Sparling, *Photographic Art* in *Orr's Circle of the Sciences: Practical Chemistry*, 1856, p.249.

[67] J. Towler, *The Silver Sunbeam*, 1864. Reprint: Morgan & Morgan, N.Y., 1969, p.130.

[68] Marcus Sparling, *Photographic Art* in *Orr's Circle of the Sciences: Practical Chemistry*, 1856, p.109.

[69] ibid., p.254.

[70] The lot description in the 2000 catalogue gives Wild Darrell as the winner of the 1856 Derby. This is a typographical error. On p.8 of the introductory essay he is correctly given as the 1855 winner.

[71] Thomas Henry Taunton, *Portraits of Celebrated Racehorses*, 1887, pp.141–144.

[72] Bombardier.

[73] So described in Mortimer, Onslow and Willett, *Biographical Encyclopaedia of British Flat Racing*, 1978, p.657.

[74] Thomas Henry Taunton, *Portraits of Celebrated Racehorses*, 1887, p.143.

[75] *The Poetical Works of Sir Walter Scott: With A Memoir Of The Author*, Boston, 1857, vol. IV, pp.230–31 and Appendix - Note P. The author is obliged to Dr Paul Barnaby of the Walter Scott Digital Archive for drawing his attention to this reference.

[76] Bodleian, *Catalogue of the Papers of Lady Clarendon*. Ms. Eng. c 2112.

[77] Thomas Henry Taunton, *Portraits of Celebrated Racehorses*, 1887, pp.143–144. which quotes the Daily Telegraph of 13th March 1866.

[78] Bodleian, *Catalogue of the Papers of Lady Clarendon*. Ms. Eng. c 2106.

[79] ibid., Ms. Eng. c 2109.

[80] Quoted from John Hannavy, *Roger Fenton of Crimble Hall*, London, 1975, pp.50–51.

[81] Valerie Lloyd, *Roger Fenton, Photographer of the 1850s*, catalogue of the exhibition at the Hayward Gallery, London, 1988, p.14.

[82] Bombardier.

[83] Bodleian, *Catalogue of the Papers of Lady Clarendon*. Ms. Eng. c 2106 (all three passages).

[84] ibid., Ms. Eng. c 2108.

[85] *Country Life*, 4th December 1909.

[86] University Library, Cambridge, Dept. of Manuscripts, Add. 8170/25.

[87] Robert Hunt, *A Manual of Photography*, 5th edn., 1857, p.131. Hunt describes Archer's design.

[88] John Wheeley Gough Gutch, *Recollections and Jottings of a Photographic Tour, Undertaken During the Years 1856-7* in *Photographic Notes* (Journal of the Birmingham Photographic Society) Vol II, No. 60, p.230.

[89] Larry J. Schaaf, *The Photographic Art of William Henry Fox Talbot*, Princeton University Press, 2000, p.254, note 5 to plate 84, quotes from Herschel to Talbot, 1937-4960, October 1847, NMPFT, document 06024, and Talbot to Herschel 26th October 1847, HS17:319, The Royal Society of London, document 06031. (Schaaf's abbreviations in the text observed).

[90] Horne and Thornthwaite, *A Guide to Photography*, 5th edn., 1852, pp.22–23.

[91] Sylvie Aubenas, in *Gustave Le Gray, 1820–1884*, original edn. Bibliothèque nationale de France, Paris 2002, this edn. in English translation, Getty Publications, Los Angeles, 2002, A '*University*' of Photography pp.31–40.

[92] ibid., *Signatures, Stamps, and Commercial Marks*, pp.353–4.

[93] Nadar: *Quand j'étais Photographe*, Paris, 1900, p.203. (Present author's translation).

[94] Barthélémy Jobert, *From the Point of View of Painting*, in *Gustave Le Gray, 1820–1884*, original edn. Bibliothèque nationale de France, Paris 2002, this edn. in English translation, Getty Publications, Los Angeles, 2002, p.233.

[95] William Vaughan: *Friedrich*, Phaidon 'Art & Ideas' series, London, 2004, p.314.

[96] From the diary note of Alexander Turgenev on a visit to the studio of Caspar David Friedrich, 6 August 1825, quoted in *German Art for Russian Imperial Palaces*, ed. Boris Asvarishch, catalogue of an exhibition of art from the State Hermitage Museum at Somerset House, London, 2002, p.63.

[97] Bodleian, *Catalogue of the Papers of Lady Clarendon*. Ms. Eng. c 2110.

[98] Lewis Carroll, *Alice in Wonderland*, 1865, chapter one, *Down the Rabbit Hole.*

[99] Bodleian, *Catalogue of the Papers of Lady Clarendon*. Ms. Eng. c 2112.

[100] ibid., Ms. Eng. c 2109.

[101] ibid., Ms. Eng. c 2112.

[102] ibid., Ms. Eng. c 2112.

[103] ibid., Ms. Eng. c 2112.

[104] ibid., Ms. Eng. c 2115.

[105] West Sussex Record Office, *The Maxse Papers* - this and following quotes to death of Frederick.

[106] *Memoirs of an Ex-Minister: An Autobiography by the Earl of Malmesbury*, London, 1884, vol. II, p.144.

[107] The Right Hon. Sir Herbert Maxwell, *The Life and Letters of George William Frederick Villiers, Fourth Earl of Clarendon*, London 1913, Vol. II, pp.168–169

[108] Bodleian, *Catalogue of the Papers of Lady Clarendon*. Ms. Eng. c 2111.

[109] *Memoirs of an Ex-Minister: An Autobiography by the Earl of Malmesbury*, London, 1884, vol. II, p.144.

[110] The Right Hon. Sir Herbert Maxwell, *The Life and Letters of George William Frederick Villiers, Fourth Earl of Clarendon*, London 1913, Vol. II, pp.168–169

[111] Bodleian, *Catalogue of the Papers of Lady Clarendon*. Ms. Eng. c 2121.

[112] C.R. Leslie, *Memoirs of the Life of John Constable*, Phaidon 1995 edn., p.262.

Appendix: *Gustave Le Gray and the Arrival of the Body of Admiral Bruat*

[113] University of Chicago Press, 1984, pl. 12.

[114] Confirmed in an email from Robert Koch to the author, 1st June 2003.

[115] Being the same as pl. 86 in *The Craven Photographic Collection* catalogue, Bearne's, Exeter, 6th May, 2000.

[116] Ken Jacobson, *The Lovely Sea View*, fn. 74.

[117] Ken Jacobson, *The Lovely Sea View*, fig. 12.

[118] Gus Macdonald, *Camera, Victorian Eyewitness*, London, 1979.

[119] Letter from the National Maritime Museum to G.P. Grima, 7th July 1978.

[120] Present author's translation, this and subsequent passages from the French.

[121] Indeed, the copy discovered in the Craven collection is possibly only the second copy to appear at auction in UK salerooms in thirty years. I do not have access to French saleroom records.

[122] Bibliothèque nationale catalogue no.158.

Picture Sources

Copyright in the following list of images, whether or not individually indicated, resides in each case with the person, collection, or institution whose name is appended to the image.

All efforts has been made to obtain permission to reproduce images where such permission is due. Any ommissions are unintentional and details of such ommissions should be addressed to the publishers.

Index